AF406382

Personal Security Detail Operations
Book 1

Personal Security Detail Operations, Volume 1

Mike Harland

Published by Mike Harland, 2022.

Personal Security Detail Operations
Book 1

Dedication

To my family, who have always been supportive of all my endeavors
And to all those who serve righteousness with love and perseverance

Copyright © Michael Harland 1997-2022

Copyright © Michael Harland, no part of this book may be copied, in part or fully on any media whatsoever without the permission of the author

About the Author

I was trained for 16-17 years in Karate, reaching black belt 2nd Dan in 1991. During this period, I participated in a number of karate competitions, winning gold and a number of bronze medals in competition. From 1985-1986 did my national service in the South African Defense Force (SADF), doing border duty for 9 months in the combat area (red zone/war zone). As a 20-year-old I saw my first contact (real life shooting) as a group of ANC/ SWAPO terrorist organizations attacked our base. Although it was probably SWAPO as the ANC's "Spear of the nation" army was a bit blunt and lost every contact with SA forces.

From about 1987 till the early 90's, I worked doing door duty at clubs. During this period in our country, badly behaved people normally took their punishment like a man, and that was where I had most of my street experience situations up until about 40 years of age. Personally, and in the capacity of a soldier and Close Protection Specialist I have used pistols and rifles extensively.

People mostly want to know what you based your training on and what experience you have. It is good for someone to ask because their life depends on the training they will receive from an instructor. You need to know that the person who is teaching you actually has experience in real combat. What does the person teaching you have to draw from as an instructor if he has no experience? Without a penchant for training in combat you won't have the will to succeed – you need a certain disposition that predisposes you to this.

In 1992 I developed an interest in Close Protection (CP), which was a very new occupation in the public sector in South Africa at the time. There was not much in the way of sophisticated training courses for civilians. So whenever there was a possibility to train with an instructor that knew what he was talking about, we would jump at the opportunity. During the period 1992 till 2005 I attended 4 separate CP courses and a number of other related courses such as shooting in low light, advanced foot and vehicle drills, Improvised Explosive Devices (IED) recognition, unarmed combat, knife fighting, and numerous other skills and courses not mentioned here. These instructors ranged from civilian instructors to ex Special Forces (SF) and FBI certified instructors. During my CP experience, I have looked after celebrities, businessmen, royalty and diplomats.

I was able to apply IED recognition experience in counter terrorism operations. In 2000 I was tasked to come up with a plan to minimize IEDs being placed in The V&A Waterfront Cape Town.

South Africa has a tradition of hunters and shooters because of the nature of the land and its tumultuous history over the last 300 years, where hunting and fighting were the order of the day, and this gave most South Africans a good taste of reality in combat. Therefore, it was more likely that we would be exposed to weapons living in South Africa.

In the military we dealt with all sorts of weapons and equipment, such as radar and radio communications etc. High threat CP is commonly referred to as Private Security Detail (PSD), and during 2004 the conflict in Iraq attracted a lot of PSD operators from all over the world. Having military experience and about 15 years in CP by that time, I decided it would benefit my overall abilities to get some PSD experience and training.

You soon learn it takes a determined, focused and deliberate mindset balanced with self confidence that will allow you to win in a real gunfight; there is no room for negative thoughts or thoughts that detract from the winning, orientated and focused mind.

When you train for combat in reality it helps to train instinctively and to train so you react and don't have to think about tactics because there is only time for reacting.

My experience with martial and unarmed combat spans about 38 years where I trained not just with Karate systems but also to a minor degree Aikido (which is not a self-defense system), Judo and some ground fighting. My weapons training was with various weapon systems, handguns and rifles etc. which spans about 30 years.

To better understand where my skill level was in terms of international standards, I did an advanced certificate in handgun and rifle skills to round off my weapons qualifications. This certifies a person to teach to an advanced level anywhere in the world and is internationally recognized. From approximately 1994/97 I started to develop the mobility shooting drills for handgun and rifle which you can now see on YouTube and also on Patreon see below.

During this period, I got most of my Close Protection experience and was tasked as team leader about 70 times or more. In the period 1990-1991 I studied physical education which has helped me better understand the body and how it functions. I apply this in my unarmed combat and weapons training courses.

The PSD Operational Environment

The operational environment that the PSD operator finds himself in is unique. This is due to the nature and the function of PSD operations, the function of the operator and the area of operations, which is a war zone (high threat area for CP operations). These factors put the operator in a situation where they are protecting a VIP (principal), and in protecting they have to engage the enemy, and therefore fighting (more accurately, attacking the enemy) is **not normally** part of the operational procedure for PSD or CP teams.

The numbers, in which the PSD team moves around, is also very small and therefore more vulnerable to enemy/insurgent/terrorist attacks. One of the reasons for not engaging the enemy is because of the possibility of overwhelming numbers of attackers in an ambush and the type of weapons which they will use against you, which would normally only be for military application. This means the casualties that can be caused are great, especially when the ambush is initiated by an IED followed by RPG then finished with rifle fire.

The normal adrenaline rush that would go with an attack and the extreme temperatures (35 to 45 degree Celsius) has a major effect on the operator – **it is debilitating**. You can get fatigued very quickly in these situations and **fatigue normally causes you to make mistakes therefore a high level of fitness is required. Acclimatization**, proper **fitness** levels and **tactics** that are **ingrained** will be essential for survival in such a high threat situation.

The size of a PSD team could be anything from 4 to 10 in size. This small size of a PSD team makes you more vulnerable to attack, as you do not move around undercover but in the open where you are easily seen.

If the operational area is Iraq or Afghanistan then you will find yourself in a very hot dry climate which means you can sweat profusely and not even be aware of the fact the you are losing so much liquid, it is therefore essential to carry the appropriate amount of liquid on you and carry the means to clean water when you find natural sources of water, which could be dams, irrigation ditches, swamps (marshy areas) and rivers.

Summary of operational area for PSD operations

- High threat environment for most PSD operations is what distinguishes it from normal CP work.
- Isolated from friendly forces, and only sometimes you will have backup in the form of Quick Response Force (QRF) or army Special Forces (SF) in the area, but don't count on this.
- Large numbers of enemy attackers, very well equipped. This means you can expect to be attacked with PKM's, RPG's, AK's and an **initiation device** such as IED's in some cases, with the odd grenade thrown in now and again.
- Hostile population, mostly but not always depending on where you are situated and the present political climate. For example, when I was in the north of Iraq, it was safer due to the presence of the Kurds who were attacked by the previous government's forces.
- Extreme temperatures cause fatigue quickly, and this is one of the most debilitating factors of working in the Middle East (even if you are acclimatized and reasonably fit).
- Small numbers of protectors, PSD operators. Therefore, the level at which the PSD operators work must be very high. Especially weapons skills and team tactics with regards to fighting (covering your buddy, assaulting, withdrawing etc.).
- The law with regards to PSD operations limits the types of weapons you can carry to an extent. This is why you should improvise where possible and use all the equipment available.
- The vehicles can carry large amounts of equipment but on foot you are limited (carry wisely). It would help to customize the vehicles to allow easy access to ammo and E&E bags as well as medical equipment.

Examples of your operational area if you're doing PSD in Iraq:

Keys to Successful PSD Operations

These are some of the factors that improve the PSD operations but remember each area of operations has its own challenges and threats, and which means you have to be flexible so you can adapt to each area, challenges and threats.

Management

As with all contracts, the management play a major role in the success of a contract as they guide the company and sometimes the teams in their specific roles. They will also be responsible for the threat assessment and or be in charge of the process even if it is done by another person in the company. This means that the quality of the assessment will be up to the management to ensure.

Because we are primarily concerned with preparing the individual operator to work in the high threat environment, we won't go into management styles.

Here are a few points

1. **Leadership that has combat experience,** this shows in the procedures and tactics employed and attitude of the leadership.
2. **Their primary concern** should be the safety of the operators, as when the operators are safe so will the principal be safe.
3. **Never go for inferior equipment** for the sake of money. A breakdown in a vehicle can in this case cause the death of all the occupants of that vehicle.
4. **Do not rush into a contract** without having done the planning and this takes time to do properly.
5. **The management** should know when to decline if the principal asks for the team to go to a known area of heavy enemy activity.
6. **Consider all operators suggestions** they would not be working in a war zone if they were untrained and or incompetent, otherwise there is something wrong with your selection criteria.
7. **Don't buy equipment** because it was the ***easiest to come by*** or cheap, look around for the correct equipment. If for

instance the webbing does not hold the correct amount of mags or breaks easy then it puts the operator at risk. This is where the time to do the planning comes in.

8. **Consider carefully** the following personnel
   a. **Team leaders** for the convoys, they must be experienced and **command** respect not **demand** respect. Lead from the front and show superior skills and abilities.
   b. **HQ personnel radio operators and staff that deal with tracking the convoys, you need calm people in this job**

9. **Management must not rely** on previous ranks as may have been held in the military. Remember you are now in a services industry that means each operator commands the same respect as you do.

10. **Members of the PSD** that are insecure and unable to be team players and find the need to point out others problems should be considered for extended leave (10 years would do). There are very few things as irritating as a person who thinks they know everything.

11. **It's better to have a corporal with 3 years** of experience in the area of operations than a general with no experience in this theatre of operations. Unless he's a general with lots of combat experience.

12. **Responsible leadership**
   a. That understands the situation and equips the operators for the job (armored vehicles/ not up armored or soft skinned). High capacity weapon systems (75 round drum mag) that don't jam in the sand, GPS tracking and **correct webbing** that can hold enough magazines for a prolonged contact. It must hold 6 or more mags; this is normally dictated

by the caliber of the rifle and the design of the vest.

b. Maintains standard with planned training sessions in all areas of PSD operations so that's a lot of training. You should be constantly busy with training to update and improve.

13. Ensures operators adhere to rules such as maintaining a good condition by **exercising** and practice.

Operational considerations

1. **High level of individual ability** for each PSD operator, because the team is only as good as its weakest operator. The training should be ongoing and should apply to all aspects of operations in a war zone this includes combat orientated training, intel (reconnaissance), medical, survival (E&E), familiarization with radios and vehicles, know your enemy (MO).
2. **Accurate, reliable and timely intel,** this is before you go on the contract when you do the threat assessment and as you are on the contract and adjust the threat assessment to suit the area you find yourself in.
3. Good robust **reliable equipment**, this applies to all the equipment that is issued, weapons, webbing, vehicles, BP vests (the holder has to be good quality otherwise it falls apart from frequent use), radios, computers as the desert environment can destroy them (fine dust gets in everywhere).
4. **On-going adaptation** to threats, adapting tactics to counter new threats and new MO of the terrorist organization
5. **On-going training** individual skills such as
    a. Marksmanship, use of cover and stoppage drills, tactical such as team drills this could be 2-man team drill house penetration etc.
    b. Medical training
    c. EOD normally won't be expected but you can't go wrong with a little knowledge on the subject
    d. Counter sniper operations as well as how snipers deploy so that you are able to make a more informed decision when planning your operation.
6. Reliable communications: equipment and procedures, this includes encrypted communications where possible.

7. **Operations room** staff that knows **where the operators** are at all times and **knows how to respond** to send assistance, whether it's the QRF (quick reaction force) or Med Evac.
8. **Correct work to rest ratio** 4 weeks on 2 weeks off roughly. The rest to work ratio will ensure better focus and lessen the degree of combat stress. You can go for much longer in reality, but the more time you spend under high stress, the more opportunity you have to get over worked and stressed out.
9. **Training and logistics** in most war zone environments you will have a range facility for the military to train at and these are sometimes available to the PSD operators.
   a. Obtain enough ammo for ongoing training, use any ammo available, even the low grade stuff, and keep the good quality ammo for operations.
      i. Focus on reflexive drills and tactics for urban operations
      ii. Focus on marksmanship and tactics for rural operations
   b. Driving is a major part of PSD operations and the operators should all train with the available vehicles as you never know when they will have to use the vehicle in an emergency.
      i. Focus on quick reaction to commands of team leader and driving fast out of contact area.
      ii. Do the following driving exercises
         1. Y- turn
         2. J –turn
         3. ramming
         4. push assist drills
      iii. Train basics for drivers till they do it

> without thought. These will include above tactics and procedures such as keep tank full of fuel, check vehicles for working order, test vehicle radios (channel), procedure for dropping clients and pick up.
>
> c. Have the necessary equipment for operation (operators must train with equipment it's no use just having it), NV (night ops), sniper carried in vehicle (this is a major threat since about 2005).

Important note: The golden rule for survival in a war zone is be unpredictable in your procedures and tactics. You should be thorough in your training, accurate in your assessments and flexible in your approach to problems that WILL arise.

[**Any tactic** or procedure **you use over and over again can be studied** and countered, so be flexible and look for new ways to approach problems as you go along]

Pre-training before a contract

The training done prior to a contract should be 6 weeks to 3 months to prepare the operators for working in a war zone. This may not always be possible to do because of the time constraints but should apply if possible.

This is because of the following reasons

1. They need to be physically in good shape
2. The team needs to have all the tactics they will use in contacts to be second nature and must be applied without thought.
3. The individual operators need to iron out all their weaknesses, such as marksmanship, tactics, and familiarization of equipment such as weapons, vehicles, and communications (they must understand call signs and radio procedure).
4. Familiarization and training with all equipment used. This is because when in a contact, you will do what you have ingrained in your ability, and not what you have just learnt. So if you have used an M16 all your life but now have an AK47 then your fingers will look for a safety that is not there and this cost you seconds in a contact and maybe your life.
    a. If you don't familiarize yourself with your equipment then you won't know that the AK gets very hot after shooting 3 mags rapidly. This gets so hot it is hard to hold the weapon because some of the handles are made of plastic, which doesn't help. If possible, get the AK with a wooden fore end it doesn't heat up as quickly as plastic.
    b. The heat also causes any oil to vaporize and restrict your vision and make it difficult to aim and breath.
    c. The 6-ton GMC doesn't respond as quickly as a

normal vehicle because of the weight and you therefore have to be very careful when turning.

5. Testing of all equipment in the environment they will be used might be done by other operators tasked with the testing prior to the team's deployment to make sure the equipment performs in the environment you find yourself. This is because all mechanical machinery has tolerances to sand, heat and moisture (your sweat).

6. DO NOT FIND OUT THE HARD WAY – test everything

7. Coordinated tactics and procedure: sometimes people may come from excellent units in their respective armies but haven't trained together and when the s.... hits the fan, they will react differently and put all the operators at risk.

Good equipment for PSD work

Webbing configuration bag

Chest webbing

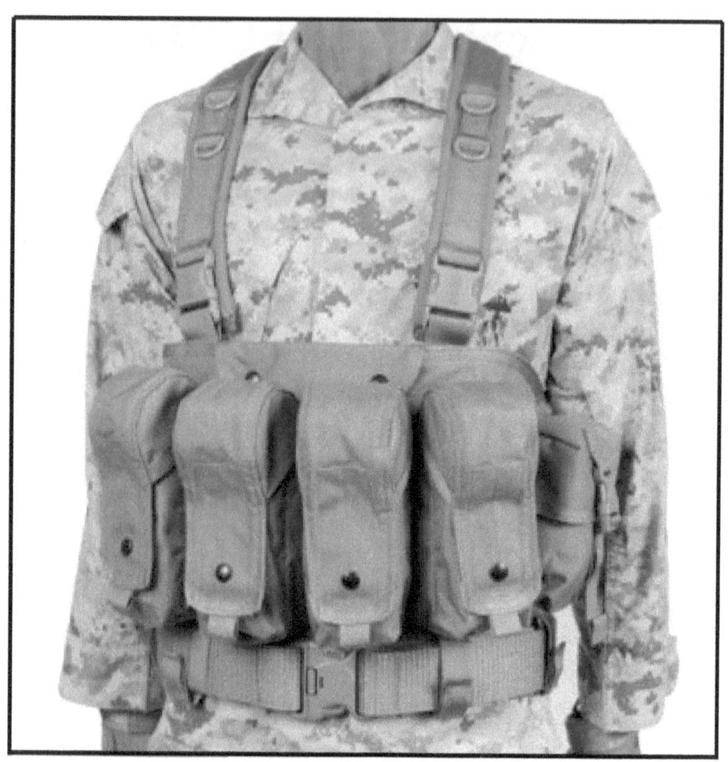

Rifle

Common mistakes in planning and PSD operations

It is always important to balance security with threat. If you consider that a normal working person that needs protection, from a person that wants to beat them, you can say is a level 1 threat and a business person who has a death threat is a level 3 to 4 threats and a head of state is a level 5 threat. The problem is, all too often that principals with a level 4 category threat don't get the protection they need, and should have according to their status.

It is important to keep in mind that when you have level 2 and 3 threats, you will control the immediate area around the principal. Persons that could be categories with level 4 and level 5 threats will have an increase in the security applied to the venue and surrounding areas. Level 5 which can be said is the highest level for civilian operations.

I think PSD operations are at a different level altogether due to the concentration of high level threats throughout the country. It's not only the number of threats but the intensity of the threats which could be assaults, IED's and sniping all in one day, but not necessarily on your principal.

Any person with a level 4 to 5 threat should have all security procedures and principles applied to them that can be applied.

Common mistakes made when planning and execution of PSD operations for level 4 and 5 categories threats

1. Not holding the high ground around the principal's arrival area and abode.
2. Not placing covert operators in the area around the arrival area and area of operations for all movements of the principal. This is only possible if you have personnel that can blend into the environment.

3. Using any form of radio communication that can be intercepted where the arrival of the principal is mentioned (this should not be done). It is stupid to think the enemy/terrorist can't figure out that the mention of a code word such as the package has arrived can easily be understood as the principal has arrived.

4. Not collecting (continuously) and **disseminating** intel as it comes in about
    a. **Changes in threat**
    b. **Changes in principal's domiciles, as they need to be searched**
    c. **Changes in team areas of control**
    d. **Changes in code words**
    e. **Changes in passwords or pass cards for personnel and visiting photographers**

5. Not controlling intel and cleaning up after leaving an area where the principal has moved through or stopped at. Nobody should know the principal's movements especially in an area where the route could have an IED placed on it if they know your specific route.

6. Not having the correct equipment to accomplish goals and objectives. This includes but is not limited to, precision rifles to control area around residence, spotter scope, binocular for counter snipers and for personnel on the ground to monitor roof tops and buildings (windows, doors etc.). This also includes debugging equipment and NV for night operations as well as thermal in certain situations. Notebooks for recording observations such as orders, call signs, danger areas, equipment, and requirements asked for by the principal, specific orders of how to deal with the press and other expected guests.

General expediency

1. Be aware
2. Wear cotton; it does not burn so easily (if you get caught in a burning vehicle)
3. Keep your E&E bag at hand
4. Keep weapons dry or very little oil in a sandy environment (one or 2 drops)
5. Have enough **ammo** and **water**
6. Check if you can move in and out of your vehicle easily; change the vehicle if you can't.
7. Know your area of operation, main routes and E&E avenues
8. Learn a bit of the local language
9. Keep up to date with latest threats
10. Keep training

General Insurgent Strategies

General strategies used by insurgents for attacks and ambushes:

1. Look out for people with video cameras for some bazaar reason they like to film you when they attack. They use the footage for political gain, instruction purpose and psychological warfare.
2. Most times they will have some sort of diversion, daisy chain alongside the road followed by RPG and AK from different angles. NB always watch your back (your "six" as some like to call it).
3. Another little trick by the enemy is to put oil on the road as you come off an off ramp. Get ready for a fight if your car starts to slide because the place you find the oil and the timing could mean an initiation for an ambush.
4. Disguised shells have been found in animal carcasses, dogs, cows and goats this will normally be left at a stop street or junction so you will have to slow down or stop.
5. Be aware of **stationary vehicles** always keep your eye on them. Sometimes stationary vehicles are just a decoy for an IED on the other side of the road. The enemy will sometimes pretend to be fixing the vehicle but the clue is if they are more interested in you than the vehicle then it's a chance they are going to do something now or planning for later.
6. Statistically the most dangerous time is between **13:00 and 18:00** (Iraq 2004 to 2005). **This may change if the insurgents/terrorist learns new ideas from other groups** coming from as far as Chechnya, Iran and other Muslim countries.
7. Driving up to a convoy and shooting from the side into the vehicle at the driver is also a common tactic followed by

people waiting in a side road to finish the job (they will either spray you with AK or RPG fire.

8. They may follow from a distance then open up on the rear vehicle as you drive along in open country, they may be as far as 100 to 200 meters. PKMs have been used (belt fed Russian made LMG).

9. During some of the ambushes the front vehicle is taken out by RPG leaving you to fight it out with guys attacking from the side or rear, keep aware of the multi directional ambushes.

10. Always be suspicious of vehicles blocking the road – never get complacent. Don't drive towards them, wherever possible take a detour and or turn around. But remember they are anticipating this so get ready to fight.

11. Be aware of decoy vehicles the side of the road, while a device is on the other side, such as HE (high explosive) shell rigged to blow as you pass, normally in a carcass or other disguised devise.

12. It is well known that the insurgents have stolen US uniforms and Hummer's, be aware. These could be used in **false roadblocks** and to gain access to facilities.

13. Watch out for the blocking car in a rolling ambush. This vehicle will pull in front of the convoy to slow it down and then have the other vehicle pull alongside and open fire.

Terrorist operations and tactics

The discussion below presents the most common types of terrorist operations and tactics. By no means is this intended to be an exhaustive discussion of this topic, since the combination of methods and approaches is virtually unlimited. However, one constant regarding terror operations is the use of techniques stressing surprise, secrecy, innovation, and indirect methods of attack. Their tactics are as broad and diverse as the imagination of the group's members. Additionally, with the use of the Internet and common training bases, terrorist groups exchange information on tactics that yield success. Al Qaeda alone has assembled in excess of 10,000 pages of written training material, hundreds of hours of training videos, and operates a worldwide network of training camps. Additionally, they have been able to field test their tactics in real-world situations since many of the terrorists have participated in conflicts such as Chechnya, Kashmir, Afghanistan, the Balkans, and Iraq.

For military professionals, a key principle to keep in mind is the difference in outlook between terror operations and military operations. The terrorist will utilize tactics, forces, and weapons specifically tailored to the particular mission. Terrorist operations are individualistic in that each is planned for a specific target and effect. Additionally, terrorists will only expose as much of their resources and personnel to capture or destruction as are absolutely necessary for mission accomplishment. A military force would approach an operation with plans to concentrate forces and keep excess combat power on hand to meet contingencies to ensure mission success and prepare for follow-on missions. A terrorist takes a minimal force and relies upon prior planning and reconnaissance to match the force, weapons, and methods to the target. There is no concept of "follow-on missions", so there is no need for redundant capability.

If changes to the target, or unexpected conditions render success unlikely, he will usually **cancel the operation** and **return later with a better weapon an updated plan or more personnel**, or whatever it may require to ensure a successful operation. For major terrorist operations, mission accomplishment will in all likelihood mean the disbanding of the force, personnel returning to their cells and covers, or forming new task groups for other operations.

In addition to adaptive and flexible organizations, terrorists also employ specific equipment built or procured for a particular operation. Because of the lag time between development of a new technology and military acquisition and fielding, terrorists can sometimes procure equipment superior to standardized military models. As an example, instead of purchasing hundreds of identical radios constructed to meet all likely uses, a terrorist will only procure the quantity he needs of the newest most capable radio appropriate for the operation. The only real limitation is funding and availability of the equipment when it is needed. Weapons will also be tailored to the particular operation. If a directional explosive is needed, the terrorist could make use of available military models of anti-tank and anti-personnel mines. Conversely, the terrorist may determine that a mine would be detected by the target's security force end route to the attack, and he therefore needs to build or obtain an alternative device. To illustrate, even counting the warheads of anti-ship cruise missiles, there was not a readily available weapon for the attack on the USS *Cole*. No one manufactures a half-ton C-4 platter charge configured to fit in a small boat, but that was exactly what the terrorists' plan required. Therefore, it was exactly what the terrorist group built. Additionally, Operation Iraqi Freedom has demonstrated the terrorists' ability to construct a variety of IED's that are effective, yet are easily emplaced and difficult to detect by military forces.

Understand the terrorist objectives

Objectives of the group conducting the operation are key to predicting likely targets. Is the intent to:

1. cause loss of faith in the authorities
2. a provocation to inspire resistance
3. to promote fear amongst the population, or
4. to inflict military casualties in an attempt to reduce national and political will?

Although several different types of operations may satisfy a particular objective, terror groups often develop expertise in one or more types of operations, and less specialization in others. Some groups will actually publish their targeting guidance. In March 2004, al Qaeda published a 9-page article in their training publication, "Camp al-Battar Magazine" that released new targeting guidance to its members and other affiliated groups. This publication contains information on everything from small arms skills, physical fitness, targeting, tactics, and secure communications. **The new guidance specifically covered targets within cities, addressing faith targets, economic targets, and human targets.**

Most common terrorist attacks

Statistically in 2004 out of 651 attacks the below mentioned were the most frequent

1. Armed attacks **314**
2. Bombing **196**
3. Kidnapping **111**

These stats give you an idea of the focus of the training and serves as a guideline as to the types of attacks to prepare for. If you cover these 3 types of attacks then you cover 621 of the attacks that were perpetrated over 2004. That means you prepare for approximately **95%** of the attacks if you train in a correct response to these types of attacks.

Although sniping is not specified in the below diagram of attacks perpetrated over the period of 2004 it would fit in under armed attacks or other, this could be as much as 30 to 50 over the period of 2004 that would make it a serious method of attack to consider and train in precautions for.

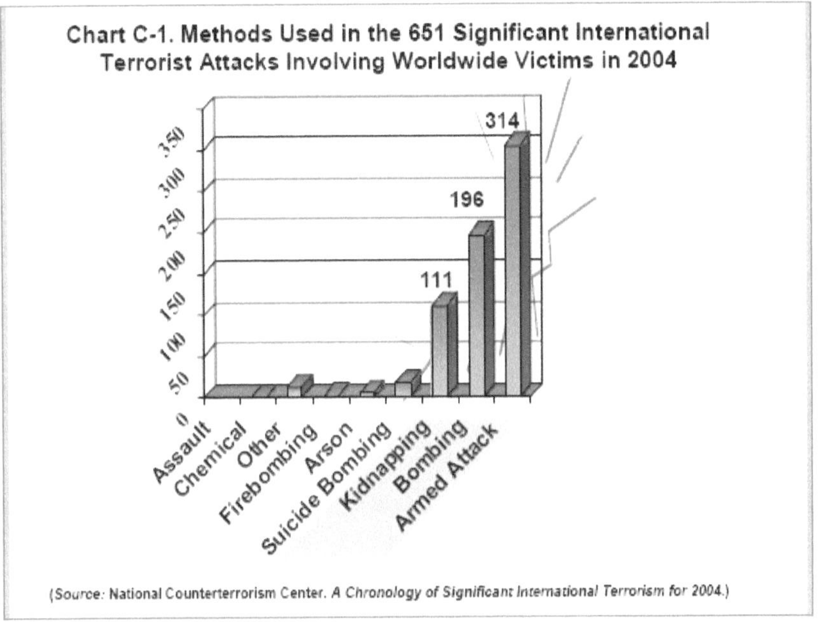

(Source: National Counterterrorism Center. *A Chronology of Significant International Terrorism for 2004.*)

IED usage in various geographic regions

34

Northern Ireland

Roadside bombs were extensively used by the terrorist group, the **Provisional IRA**[1] in Northern Ireland[2], during the Provisional IRA campaign 1969-1997[3]. A typical roadside bomb was placed in a drain or "culvert" along a rural road and exploded by remote control when British Army[4] or other security forces vehicles were passing. The most lethal example of these attacks came in 1979, when 18 British soldiers were killed by two "culvert bombs" at Warren point[5]. As a result of the use of these bombs the British military had to stop transport by road in certain areas and use helicopter transport instead. In addition, in the 1980s and 1990s, all culverts were welded and concreted shut so that explosives could not be placed in them.

The problem was not just IED's but ambushes by armed men using almost all the modern military equipment available such as assault rifles and belt fed machine guns. Sniping was also used and at one stage a 50 cal system was used to attack soldiers.

The problems in Ireland have not ended and the terrorist groups from Ireland have been suggested as a source of training for some Middle Eastern terrorist groups.

1. http://en.wikipedia.org/wiki/Provisional_IRA

2. http://en.wikipedia.org/wiki/Northern_Ireland

3. http://en.wikipedia.org/wiki/Provisional_IRA_campaign_1969-1997

4. http://en.wikipedia.org/wiki/British_Army

5. http://en.wikipedia.org/wiki/Warrenpoint

Afghanistan

Following the invasion[1] of Afghanistan[2] by the USSR[3] on 27 December[4] 1979[5], the Afghan Mujahedeen[6] were supplied with large quantities of military supplies from many Muslim[7] states and from the United States. Among those supplies were many types of anti-tank mines[8].

The Afghan Mujahedeen preferred to remove the explosives from several foreign anti-tank mines, and combine the explosives in tin cooking-oil cans for a more powerful blast. Often the foreign anti-tank mines were enclosed in plastic containers, making them difficult to detect. By combining the explosives from several mines and placing them in tin-cans, the Afghan Mujahedeen made them easier to detect. **The Afghan Mujahedeen almost always covered their mines with direct fire weapons.**

Afghan Mujahedeen operating far from the border with Pakistan[9] did not have a ready supply of foreign anti-tank mines. They preferred to make mines from Soviet unexploded ordnance.

The anti-tank mines in this conflict were rarely triggered by pressure fuses. They were almost always remotely detonated.

Since the 2001 invasion of Afghanistan[10], the Taliban[11] and its supporters have used IEDs against American, ISAF[12] and Afghan

---

1. http://en.wikipedia.org/wiki/Soviet_invasion_of_Afghanistan

2. http://en.wikipedia.org/wiki/Afghanistan

3. http://en.wikipedia.org/wiki/USSR

4. http://en.wikipedia.org/wiki/December_27

5. http://en.wikipedia.org/wiki/1979

6. http://en.wikipedia.org/wiki/Mujahideen

7. http://en.wikipedia.org/wiki/Muslim

8. http://en.wikipedia.org/wiki/Anti-tank_mine

9. http://en.wikipedia.org/wiki/Pakistan

10. http://en.wikipedia.org/wiki/2001_invasion_of_Afghanistan

military and civilian vehicles. While the number of such attacks has been far lower than those in Iraq **the number has been steadily increasing.**

11.   http://en.wikipedia.org/wiki/Taliban

12.   http://en.wikipedia.org/wiki/International_Security_Assistance_Force

Lebanon

Hezbollah[1] pioneered the use of IEDs against military forces after the 1982 invasion of Lebanon[2] by Israel[3]. Israel withdrew from most of Lebanon[4] in 1985 but still kept troops stationed in a buffer zone[5] in southern Lebanon. Hezbollah frequently used IEDs to attack Israeli vehicles in this area up until the Israeli withdrawal in May 2000[6].

One such bomb killed Israeli Brigadier General[7] Erez Gerstein[8] on February 28[9], 1999[10], the highest-ranking Israeli to die in Lebanon.

Also in the 2006 Israel-Lebanon conflict[11], a Merkava[12] Mark II tank[13] was hit by a Hezbollah[14] IED killing all 4 IDF[15] servicemen on board, the first of two IED's damaging a Merkava[16] tank

1. http://en.wikipedia.org/wiki/Hezbollah

2. http://en.wikipedia.org/wiki/1982_invasion_of_Lebanon

3. http://en.wikipedia.org/wiki/Israel

4. http://en.wikipedia.org/wiki/Lebanon

5. http://en.wikipedia.org/wiki/Buffer_zone

6. http://en.wikipedia.org/wiki/May_2000

7. http://en.wikipedia.org/wiki/Brigadier_General

8. http://en.wikipedia.org/w/index.php?title=Erez_Gerstein&action=edit

9. http://en.wikipedia.org/wiki/February_28

10. http://en.wikipedia.org/wiki/1999

11. http://en.wikipedia.org/wiki/2006_Israel-Lebanon_conflict

12. http://en.wikipedia.org/wiki/Merkava

13. http://en.wikipedia.org/wiki/Tank

14. http://en.wikipedia.org/wiki/Hezbollah

15. http://en.wikipedia.org/wiki/IDF

16. http://en.wikipedia.org/wiki/Merkava

Chechnya

IEDs have also been popular in Chechnya[1], where Russian[2] forces are currently engaged in fighting with rebels. While no concrete statistics are available on this matter bombs have accounted for many Russian deaths in both the

- **First Chechen War**[3] **(1994[4]-1996[5])**
- The **Second**[6] **Chechen war (1999[7]-2008).**

1. http://en.wikipedia.org/wiki/Chechnya

2. http://en.wikipedia.org/wiki/Russia

3. http://en.wikipedia.org/wiki/First_Chechen_War

4. http://en.wikipedia.org/wiki/1994

5. http://en.wikipedia.org/wiki/1996

6. http://en.wikipedia.org/wiki/Second_Chechen_War

7. http://en.wikipedia.org/wiki/1999

Iraq

Beginning in **July 2003**[1], the Iraqi insurgency[2] used IEDs—more often referred to as roadside bombs by the press—to target American and Coalition[3] vehicles.

Common locations for placing these bombs in include

1. Animal[4] carcasses[5]
2. Soda cans
3. Boxes[6].
4. Where the road curves
5. Where the road narrows (bridge)

Typically, they explode underneath or to the side of the vehicle to cause the maximum amount of damage.

However, as vehicle armor[7] was improved on military vehicles, insurgents began placing IEDs in elevated positions such as

1. On **road signs**[8]
2. Bridges
3. **Trees**[9], in order to hit less protected areas.

---

1. http://en.wikipedia.org/wiki/July_2003

2. http://en.wikipedia.org/wiki/Iraqi_insurgency

3. http://en.wikipedia.org/wiki/Multinational_force_in_Iraq

4. http://en.wikipedia.org/wiki/Animal

5. http://en.wikipedia.org/wiki/Carcass

6. http://en.wikipedia.org/wiki/Box

7. http://en.wikipedia.org/wiki/Vehicle_armor

8. http://en.wikipedia.org/wiki/Traffic_sign

9. http://en.wikipedia.org/wiki/Tree

Most of the IEDs in Iraq are made with artillery[10] or mortar[11] shells[12] attached to a detonator[13], but sometimes they are made with large amounts of explosives[14].

IEDs have accounted for (as of October 2005) about **one-third of all American deaths** in Iraq. Despite the increased armor[15], IEDs have been killing soldiers with greater frequency; in a ten month period in 2005, **302** U.S. soldiers were killed by such devices.

According to the Pentagon, **250,000 tons (of 650,000 tons total)** of Iraqi ordnance were looted, providing a nigh endless source of ammunition for the insurgents. In October 2005[16], Britain[17] charged that Iran[18] was supplying insurgents with the technological know-how to make shaped charges[19], which focus the blast upwards and can pierce even the most heavily armored vehicles. Iran has denied this allegation, but we know they have the expertise and motive. Recently IEDs have been deployed in the form of Explosively Formed Penetrators[20] a special type of shaped charge that is effective at long standoffs from the target (50 meters or more). These are especially problematic to counter because they can be emplaced so far from their intended targets.

Another possibility is platter charges. **Platter charges** are rectangular or circular pieces of flat metal (usually steel) with plastic explosives pressed onto one side of the platter. The amount of explosive

---

10.   http://en.wikipedia.org/wiki/Artillery

11.   http://en.wikipedia.org/wiki/Mortar_(weapon)

12.   http://en.wikipedia.org/wiki/Projectile

13.   http://en.wikipedia.org/wiki/Detonator

14.   http://en.wikipedia.org/wiki/Explosive

15.   http://en.wikipedia.org/wiki/Armor

16.   http://en.wikipedia.org/wiki/October_2005

17.   http://en.wikipedia.org/wiki/Britain

18.   http://en.wikipedia.org/wiki/Iran

19.   http://en.wikipedia.org/wiki/Shaped_charge

20.   http://en.wikipedia.org/wiki/Explosively_Formed_Penetrator

used is usually equal by weight to the weight of the platter. The explosives propel the platter into the target. The **effective range can be as far as 50 meters.**

The British also accused Iran and Hezbollah[21] of teaching Iraqi fighters to use infrared[22] light beams to trigger IEDs as this is very effective at disabling convoys. As the occupation forces become more sophisticated in interrupting radio signals around their convoys, the Iraqis adapt their triggering methods. Thus far the British have failed to present any evidence to substantiate their charges.

---

21.   http://en.wikipedia.org/wiki/Hezbollah

22.   http://en.wikipedia.org/wiki/Infrared

Effectiveness of terrorist attacks

Below is an example of how terrorism can affect a major power. Terrorism has become one of the most pervasive and critical threats to the security of the United States in recent history. U.S. military fatalities from terrorist actions between 1980 and 2002 exceed the total battle deaths from Operations Urgent Fury (Grenada), Just Cause (Panama), and Desert Shield/Desert Storm (Persian Gulf).3 As Chart Intro-1 depicts active duty U.S. military deaths between 1980 and 2002, there were 672 military deaths attributed to either hostile action or terrorism. Of these deaths, 63% were due to terrorist actions. Since these Department of Defense figures only go through 2002, they do not include the most current casualties from Operation Enduring Freedom (OEF), or any of the casualties from Operation Iraqi Freedom (OIF). However, sampling reports on OEF5 and OIF6 present casualties and causes, with many of the casualties caused by terrorist actions in these two theaters.

Recent statistics for 2005 illustrate a significant number of coalition military deaths in Iraq caused by acts of terrorism via vehicle borne improvised explosive devices or other suicide attacks. On occasion, adversary combatant forces have adopted terrorist tactics to continue their fight when they no longer possess the ability or choice to conduct conventional engagement attacks. In the 2003 State Department

Patterns of Global Terrorism Report, the State Department did make a distinction between military operations and terrorist attacks. Those attacks directed at combatants are not classified as terrorist attacks, whereas those against noncombatants (civilians and military personnel who at the time of the incident were unarmed and/or not on duty) were classified as terrorist attacks. Discrete measurement of terrorist effects on military forces becomes more difficult as forms of conflict overlap or merge during the conduct of operations. Regardless of how casualties are officially categorized, terrorism has been a major threat to the security of our armed forces for a number of years.

Historical background to terrorism

From history we can see that after the 2nd WW you had a Russian army that had built itself up to a massive extent with armaments and weapons. This combined with the desire by the Russian leadership to be a world power lead to what seems to be expansion by any means of terrorism, this been combined with communist ideology. This is also as a matter of the last 200 years of history that has molded the Russian mindset that after being attacked by Napoleon and Hitler, they should protect themselves against further aggression by building up their defenses (or this is what we are lead to believe). This coincides with the founding of the state of Israel, which the Arab world did not want, or this is what we are lead to believe? This was a threat to Arab power in the region and they saw this part of the world as theirs this area being the whole Middle East. With weapons and explosives in abundance which was easy to obtain with the control and access to these weapons not well balanced with the destructive power of them.

Borders and checkpoints were not well controlled and it was easy for people to cross over into another country and carry on activity as they wished, activity such as subversion and terrorism which is most probably the whole intention of the communist agenda all along. The fact that there were a lot of people who had taken part in the second WW did not help either. The training establishments were still in operation and are easy to adapt.

Over the period of 1965 to 1980 you saw a worldwide increase in terrorism on almost every continent. I am sure **this is no accident** and was a planned situation by the communist governments that sought to expand their power and to take over by disrupting things as much as possible. Although it seems as though it started in earnest in 1965 it was more likely the seeds were sown much earlier as early as the 1920's. This could have been due to the abundance of weapons and training made available by the 1st WW and the war had a destabilizing effect on the countries all over Europe and Middle East.

With the local agendas of the Muslim nations, wanting their form of government and way of life established, on a worldwide stage, but first locally. This with the communist agenda fueling the flames of insurgencies worldwide wherever it could be done helped add to the problem.

At this time it was of strategic importance for the US to counter the advance by the USSR. Supplying finances and logistics to those opposing the USSR did this.

One of the first examples of coordinated large scale uses of IED's was Belarusian 'Rail War' launched by Belarusian guerillas against the Nazis during **World War II**[1]. Both command detonated and delayed-fuse IEDs were used to derail thousands of Nazi trains during 1943-1944.

---

1.   http://en.wikipedia.org/wiki/World_War_II

Countries linked to terrorist training

A few Countries that have known or suspected links to training terrorist

47

1. Russia
2. Cuba
3. Libya
4. Iran
5. Ireland (not the country but the IRA)
6. North Korea

Theatre-specific Threats to PSD Operations

The training is also geared towards giving the student ways of dealing with these threats and managing the general security situation around the principal.

General background

The threats studied in this section are predominantly found in war zones, but not only in war zones. The threat from IED snipers and ambushes are relevant to all Close Protection jobs. It is the intensity with which you find these attacks taking place that make the difference.

Although the major threats will be addressed, this is not to say the other threats will not be a concern as well. We will just address the major threats for the sake of time, as these are more likely to happen than the other smaller attacks. It must be kept in mind that the other methods of attacks are relevant as well.

Trends in IED deployment and design change, sniper tactics change, as well as assault tactics. And are dynamic. No threat ever remains the same, as the dynamic of combat is that it's forever changing, as one combatant looks for a weakness in their enemies, tactical procedures and abilities.

What does this mean to you as an operator?

Just this: BE CREATIVE AND DONT BE PREDICTABLE.

Security report

Security reports are essential to understand the theatre of operations. For example, we'll look at the Iraqi situation.

Background knowledge to Iraqi Insurgency Groups

The insurgency in Iraq has grown in size and complexity over the course of 2004. Attacks numbered **approximately 25 per day** at the **beginning** of 2004, and averaged in the **60's by the end of the year**. Insurgents demonstrated their ability to increase attacks around key events such as the Iraqi Interim Government (IIG) transfer of power, Ramadan and the January 2005 election. Attacks on Iraq's Election Day reached approximately 300(double the previous one day high of approximately 150 reached during Ramadan 2004).

The pattern of attacks remains the same as in 2004. **Approximately 80%** of all attacks occur **in Sunni-dominated central Iraq**. The **Kurdish north** and **Shi'a south** remain relatively calm.

Coalition Forces continue to be the primary targets. Iraqi Security Forces and Iraqi Interim Government (IIG) officials are attacked to intimidate the Iraqi people and undermine control and legitimacy. **Attacks against foreign nationals are intended to intimidate non-government organizations and contractors and inhibit reconstruction and economic recovery**. Attacks against the country's infrastructure, especially electricity and the oil industry, are intended to stall economic recovery, increase popular discontent and further undermine support for the IIG and Coalition.

The exact elements attacking the US-led coalition's nation-building effort remain unclear. Since the declared end to major combat operations on 1 May 2003, the continuing attacks against Coalition troops, **civilian contractors**, **aid workers**, new Iraqi security forces, as well as the infrastructure, have undermined efforts to reconstruct and stabilize the country. They carried the total American troop fatality level over 1,000, and led many in the U.S. and elsewhere to question whether the country can be pacified at all, without a longer commitment than most consider palatable.

Attention has been paid to Saddam loyalists, Iraqi nationalists, foreign Jihadists, militant Sunni and Shi'a Muslims, and ordinary criminals, with officials trying to assess the nature, goals, funding, and capabilities of the insurgents, the degree of cooperation or conflict between the groups, and links between the insurgency and international terrorist networks and foreign governments.

On 14 November 2003 General John Abizaid, the head of US Central Command, estimated the number of fighters operating against US and allied forces at no more than 5,000, and said the insurgency remained a 'loosely organized operation'. Abizaid said "there is some level of cooperation that's taking place at very high levels, although I'm not sure I'd say there's a national-level resistance leadership." He also said "the most dangerous enemy to us at the present time are the former regime loyalists" operating in central Iraq.

According to Abizaid, "The goal of the enemy ... is not to defeat us militarily, because they don't have the wherewithal to defeat us militarily. The goal of the enemy is to break the will of the United States of America. It's clear, it's simple, and it's straightforward. Break our will; make us leave before Iraq is ready to come out and be a member of the responsible community of nations."

Almost a year on, with kidnappings and beheadings by Islamic militants, large cities still not under the control of coalition forces and months away from planned elections, with security problems requiring the diversion of funds from reconstruction projects, assumptions were being reconsidered and estimates revised.

The New York Times reported on 22 October 2004 that senior American officials believed that **"hard-core resistance"** comprised between **8,000 and 12,000** people, with the number jumping above **20,000** when "active **sympathizers or covert accomplices are included."**

Moreover, officials believed around **50 militant cells** were **drawing on "unlimited money"** through **underground networks** supplied by people connected with the former regime, as well as **wealthy Saudis and Islamic charities**. Though some groups had the ability to carry out attacks in regions other than their own, and there may be some degree of cooperation between regions, it is believed that insurgent activities are organized regionally and that no national insurgent network exists.

In January 2005 Iraqi Intelligence Service Director General Mohamed Abdullah Shahwani said that Iraq's insurgency consisted of at least 40,000 hardcore fighters, out of a total of more than 200,000 part-time fighters and volunteers who provide intelligence, logistics and shelter. Shahwani said the resistance enjoyed wide backing in the Sunni provinces of Baghdad, Babel, Salahuddin, Diyala, Nineveh and Tamim. Shahwani said the Baath, with a core fighting strength of more than 20,000, had split into three factions. The main one, still owing allegiance to jailed dictator Saddam Hussein, is operating out of Syria. It is led by Saddam's half-brother Sabawi Ibrahim al-Hassan and former aide Mohamed Yunis al-Ahmed, who provide funding to their connections in Mosul, Samarra, Baquba, Kirkuk and Tikrit. Izzat Ibrahim al-Duri is still in Iraq. Two other factions have broken from Saddam, but have yet to mount any attacks. Islamist factions range from Abu Musab al-Zarqawi's al-Qaeda affiliate to Ansar al-Sunna and Ansar al-Islam.

A picture of the composition of the insurgency, though in constant flux, has come into somewhat greater focus. London-based International Institute for Strategic Studies estimates roughly 1,000 foreign Islamic jihadists have joined the insurgency. There is no doubt, many of these have had a dramatic effect on perceptions of the insurgency through high-profile video-taped kidnappings and beheadings. However, American officials believe that the greatest obstacles to stability are the native insurgents that predominate in the Sunni triangle. Significantly, many secular Sunni leaders were being surpassed in influence by Sunni militants. This development mirrors the rise of **militant Shi'a cleric and militia leader** Moqtada al-Sadr vis-à-vis the more moderate Shi'a cleric Grand Ayatollah al-Sistani.

Still, the New York Times article also references military data suggesting roughly 80 percent of violent attacks in Iraq were simply criminal in nature –e.g., ransom kidnappings and hijacking convoys- and without political motivation. This figure lends credence to those who cited the CPA's disbanding of the Iraqi army as an error likely to create a pool of unemployed and discontented young males ripe for absorption into the insurgency. Further, this statistic highlights the importance of reconstruction, and the revitalization of an economy in Iraq that can provide traditional employment opportunities. Of the remaining 20 percent of violent attacks –those with political motivation- four-fifths are believed attributable to native insurgents as opposed to foreigners.

In late July 2005, Gen. Jack Keane, a former deputy chief of staff for the Army, said that **US and Iraqi forces** had **killed or captured** over **50,000 Iraqi insurgents since the beginning of 2005**. The Pentagon had been previously stated that 15,000 to 16,000 Iraqis were in custody in Iraq. The difference is explained by the fact that some Iraqis who were detained in military operations were subsequently released.

Former Regime Loyalists [FRL]

Sunni Arabs, dominated by Baathist and Former Regime Elements (FRE), comprise the core of the insurgency. Baathist/FRE and Sunni Arab networks are likely collaborating, providing funds and guidance across family, tribal, religious and peer group lines.

The Former Regime Loyalists or FRL's, threatened the safety of Iraqis and prolong the Coalition presence. By capturing the FRL's, US Forces are helping Iraq move forward to a peaceful and prosperous future. Baathist loyalists are thought to be responsible for some of the recent attacks against U.S. forces. According to 21 July 2003 Newsweek, two months before the war began, the Mukhabarat, the Iraqi secret police, issued instructions, "to do what's necessary after the fall of the Iraqi leadership to the American-British-Zionist Coalition forces, God forbid..."

The document outlined a total of 11 steps which were to be taken if the U.S. overthrew Saddam's regime. These included

1. Looting and burning government institutions.
2. In addition, it included orders to sabotaging power plants,
3. Creating chaos by utilizing stolen weapons.

The Pentagon has not officially verified this document, according to Newsweek, but has called it "plausible." The current sabotage and attacks seem to substantiate the possibility that Baathist loyalists are responsible for some of the mayhem.

In addition, L. Paul Bremer may have unleashed these former soldiers against US Troops by disbanding the Iraqi military. These former Guard members are without any income, but still are armed and ready to kill, making US Troops vulnerable to attack. While the Republican Guard experienced high casualties in the US strikes on Baghdad, the **Special Republican Guard** was not especially involved in this part of the war, **allowing them to disappear with a number of weapons and munitions. Approximately 40,000 men were members of the Republican Guard.**

According to the 12 August 2003 New York Times, there is an estimated 100,000 former Iraqi security service members without employment, mostly concentrated in the Sunni Triangle, the same region where many of the attacks have occurred.

Islamic Revivalist

Muslims have been oppressed for decades under the rule of Saddam Hussein. While extremist elements are inexperienced in planning attacks, other regional groups are sure to come to their assistance.

Such groups include the

1. Al- Faruq Brigades, a militant wing of the Islamic Movement in Iraq (Al-Harakah al-Islamiyyah fi al-arak),
2. the Mujahedeen of the Victorious Sect (Mujahedeen al ta'ifa al-Mansoura)
3. The Mujahedeen Battalions of the Salafi Group of Iraq (Kata'ib al mujahedeen fi al-jama'ah al-salafiyah fi al-'arak);
4. The Jihad Brigades/Cell.

Another insurgency group called "White Flags, Muslim Youth and Army of Mohammed" have claimed responsibility for the attacks against U.S. Forces. The White Flags have urged other Iraqis to attack Americans. In a 10 August 2003 videotape aired on the satellite network Al Arabiya, a Dubai-based station, the White Flags announced that the only way to free Iraq from American occupiers was through guerilla war. "We want to warn countries of the world for the last time not to send troops into Iraq."

Ansar al Islam, a Taliban-like, jihadist group with tie to Al Qaeda is also suspected in guerilla attacks. Before Operation Iraqi Freedom, it was estimated to have **850 members**, but nearly **200 were killed by Kurdish and U.S. Special Forces** in March. An estimated **300 to 350 fled to Iran** during Iraqi freedom, after a few hundred surrendered or were captured.

The 07 May 2003 bombing of the Jordanian Embassy in Iraq has added to speculation that Islamic revivalists, like Ansar al Islam, may be playing a stronger role in the Iraqi insurgency than originally estimated.

L. Paul Bremer, the civilian administrator for Iraq, has publically speculated that Ansar al Islam may have been responsible for the car bombing. The attack killed 19 people and wounded more than 60.

One group of Ansar al-Islam militants captured in the Kurdish region during early August 2003 consisted of five Iraqis, a Palestinian and a Tunisian. It was reported that the men had five forged Italian passports for another group of militants. It is estimated that at least 150 members of Ansar al-Islam have entered Iraq with the help of smugglers within the last few weeks.

Of the tens of thousands of unemployed former Iraqi security service members, an estimated 2,000 of them, most especially those without any source of income at all, are likely to be recruited by Islamic fundamentalist groups, like Ansar al-Islam.

Recruitment of militants

Recruiting militants has been observed to take place in three stages.

1. First, there is some form of contact initiated, perhaps in a mosque after daily prayers.
2. In this first conversation, a later meeting is arranged. After this meeting, some of the prospective militants are eliminated,
3. Leaving the third round of candidates that will train in the campus. According to the 12 August 2003 New York Times, these recruits are instructed to move away from their families and terminate communication with all outsiders.

Foreign fighters are a small component of the insurgency and comprise a very small percentage of all detainees. **Syrian**, **Saudi**, **Egyptian**, **Jordanian** and **Iranian** nationals make up the majority of foreign fighters. Fighters, arms and other *supplies continue to enter Iraq from virtually all of its neighbors* despite increased border security.

Syrian and Iranian involvement

In December 2004 **US General George Casey** warned that sympathizers of the insurgency within Syria had been allowed to provide funding, weapons and information to Iraqi insurgents and continued to be a source of infiltration by foreign volunteers. The following February, Iraqi television broadcast taped confessions of alleged insurgents, who claimed to have been trained in Syria, possibly by Syrian intelligence officials. Yet while coalition forces often suspect Syria of assisting insurgents, Syrian denials are adamant and hard evidence is lacking.

Also in February, after continued American pressure, Syria delivered Sabawi Ibrahim Hassan, a half-brother of Saddam and a financial backer of the insurgency.

US officials reported some improvement in co-operation against the insurgency from Syria, whose border forces are too few to police the porous Iraqi border effectively. While coalition-aided Iraqi border controls are strengthening, **Iraq's borders**, totaling **3,650 kilometers** in length, remain difficult to control.

As with Syria, the Iranian presence in Iraq is difficult to gauge, although it certainly exists. Several Shiite political parties (including SCIRI and al-Da'wa, both members of the United Iraqi Alliance, the country's dominant political coalition), have ties to Iran. The Interim Iraqi Government repeatedly expressed concern over Iraqi influence, Defense Minister Hazem Sha'alan claiming in mid-2004 that there was "clear interference in Iraqi issues by Iran" and that the latter supported terrorism in Iraq. The recalcitrant cleric Muqtada al-Sadr is widely perceived as an Iranian proxy, while in a television interview, **Muayed al-Nasseri**, commander of Saddam's "Army of Muhammad," said his **group received weapons and cash from both Iran and Syria.**

Operational intent of terrorism

Terrorism is a psychological act that communicates through the medium of violence or the threat of violence. Terrorist strategies will be aimed at publicly causing damage to symbols or inspiring fear. Timing, location, and method of attacks accommodate media dissemination and ensure "newsworthiness" to maximize impact. A terrorist operation will often have the goal of manipulating popular perceptions, and will achieve this by controlling or dictating media coverage. This control need not be overt, as terrorists analyze and exploit the dynamics of major media outlets and the pressure of the "News cycle."

A terrorist attack that appears to follow this concept was the bombing of commuter trains in Madrid, Spain in March 2004. There has been much speculation as to the true objective behind these bombings. One view is that Islamic terrorists who specifically planned to influence the political process in Spain conducted the attacks. They believed that the large percentage of the Spanish population opposed the war in Iraq and would feel that the current government was responsible for the bombings, and would therefore vote for the opposition. The attacks occurred during morning rush hour just three days prior to national elections. The timing facilitated maximum casualties on the trains (killing 191 people and injuring more than 1800), plus immediate news coverage throughout the world of the carnage resulting from this terrorist attack.

Although it cannot definitively be linked to the bombings, an anti-war Socialist prime minister was elected who quickly withdrew Spain's military forces from Iraq. In considering possible terrorist targets, recognize that a massively destructive attack launched against a target that cannot or will not attract sufficient media coverage to impact the target audience is not a viable target for terrorists. A small attack against a "media accessible" target is better than a larger one of less publicity. However, the spread of the global media makes many locations attractive targets that would not have been remotely considered thirty or forty years ago.

Preparation for High Threat Operations

This subject deals with how to get ready for working in a high threat environment and with all combat tasks all aspects should be considered which include physical (exercise), mental (mindset), tactical (foot and vehicle tactics) and procedures.

It should be considered that although the ideas of what training, needs to be done for high threat contracts is dependent on the objectives of the company and the reason for being in the PSD environment. If the company's sole function is to escort VIP's around then all aspects of driving and anti-ambush drills as well as countering all the other threats in the PSD environment. If the threat was going too countered while guarding the premises inside of the protected areas then the security training will revolve around static guarding and managing the access points of the compound.

So, the points made below are more for actual PSD operations and for other aspects of working in a war zone environment.

Methods of attack for High Threat Areas

Specific threats, or predominant methods of attacks are:

1. IED's, placed on road side are the most numerous type
2. Suicide bombers on foot (see case study on Palestine)
3. VBIED's see power point presentation.
4. Assault (ambush)
5. Sniper attacks
6. Abductions

Statistics and trends

1. Types of devices
2. Method of delivery (how the device gets to the objective)
3. Operations and surveillance
4. Ambush/abduction/seizure/suicide bomber/assassination

Specific threats

65

Preparation phases for High Threat contracts

1. The contract phase where the agreement between the company and client are discussed. This will determine the
   a. Specific function of the company e.g. close protection, static guarding, advisors etc.
   b. Budget
2. The threat assessment (you can divide your assessment up in the following way)
   a. Preliminary assessment will deal with the country as a whole, with general problems such as crime, government, military police situation, weather; geography (major roads and rivers) looked at.
   b. Final assessment will be more specific to the principal.
3. The threat will determine the sort of personnel you will be using, as in Iraq and Afghanistan it will normally be people with a previous military experience.
4. The PSD Company will establish what they need to do to address the specific needs of working in a high threat environment.
   a. The threat and budget will determine the limit of the training (how much is available)
   b. The equipment is also dictated by threat and budget
5. Once all the planning and preparation has been done then the actual training for the contract will begin but does not stop there, as training to survive in a high threat environment is an ongoing affair.

General training goals for working in high threat environments

To increase survival skills threat recognition should be paramount.
You need creative ways to improve the operator's awareness.

1. Awareness is your first line of defense and this should be reiterated continuously.
2. This includes scanning the crowd (body language)
3. Understanding specifics of the attacks by local groups/insurgents (MO).

Increasing reflexes and reaction time with all weapons systems.

1. speed drills (doing the draw or rifle presentation as fast as possible)
2. competition amongst the guys

Refining the basics of weapons skill.

1. Grip
   a. stance
   b. trigger control
   c. follow up shots
2. Movement (the basis for all combat) one of the most neglected physical skills.
3. Point aim
4. fast target acquisition (how fast you get the sight picture in front of your eyes and on target)
5. magazine changes
6. stoppage drills.

Keep the tactics basic and focus more on individual skill initially then team drills later on when individual skills are up to standard.

Mental focus and physical relaxation: these skills do not come naturally to some people and should be practiced constantly to get the person to be able to apply them in a combat environment

1. mindset
2. mental tools
3. mental rehearsal.

Use peripheral vision stimulation drills to increase awareness and open up the vision for combat so you won't experience the narrow focus that comes with combat. This is one of the most important drills to enhance your ability in close quarter combat but is probably one of the most ignored as people don't understand its application.

Then we have soft focus which is your ability to not only focus on an attacker but the person next to him as well simultaneously.

Include scanning drills to all exercises

1. The 'z' pattern
2. Figure 8
3. Left and right.
4. Close and far

Individual coaching benefits

Individual coaching by a combat instructor to improve each person's skill is more important than team tactics.

1. Only once each person's skill is at an appropriate level can the team be affective as a whole, otherwise a weak link can bring the whole team down in a contact.
2. Consider the person watching your six, if they are unable to engage the enemy effectively.

Encourage flexibility and improvisation

1. A combat situation is dynamic and changing.
2. You will never have the same situation in combat something always changes and this means you should have the flexibility that allows you to prevail.
3. Flexibility should apply to all areas such as counter surveillance, vehicle drills, SOP's
4. Many techniques and tactics used now in the two most dangerous war zones were only applied once they got to these places.

Start slowly to familiarize yourself with the dynamics of what you are doing; this will also help when you go faster. This is a proven sound training principle for all levels of operator. This includes all physical drills such as weapons training, unarmed combat, driving skills etc.

Preparation logistical and expertise

Without the very basic preparation, you are planning to fail. For example, good planning would include but is not limited to:

1. Good quality functional weapons
2. Properly armored vehicles (not up-armored ones)
3. Appropriate maps of area of operations and mapping programs (these are not discussed as each person must decide what they will use). The maps must allow have enough details to see the terrain to plan routes. These are helped by using Google earth maps where needed.
4. **Team training** to **familiarize each person with the other operator's skills** and **tactics** you cannot hope to run a professional team and get the results that come with proper preparation. This is because most of the time you will work with operators from 2 or 3 or more different countries.
5. Mechanic (Workshop) facility to fix vehicles and make changes to the vehicles like take the back armored window out to allow shooting from this vehicle. If you don't have a mechanic workshop then you should have at least 2 extra vehicles, as they could get damaged in a contact.
6. You should have medically trained staff to deal with major trauma situation and minor cuts and bruises that will come from working in rough environment stuff. Level 7 medics are more applicable to working in such a high threat environment.
7. Accommodation should be strengthened to take incoming mortar rounds and rifle rounds as well fragmentation from an IED as these go off even inside a secure compound.
8. Have the correct staff for the threats you will find in your area of operations such as EOD, counter sniper (more and more

important), drivers, advanced shooters for the Close Protection, intel officer that understand collection/ interpretation and how to disseminate.

This is not even taking into consideration good tactics or adapting your drills to suit the environment.

Team Construction of a PSD Operation

When working in a high threat environment you will want to address as many areas of security when looking after a principal as possible. There will always be budgetary restraints and clients' personal likes and dislikes to overcome, whether it's a government that you are working for or a private person or company.

The areas that will be discussed in this document are some of the areas that will need to be considered when working in such an environment. With all Close Protection contracts you will want to apply as many aspects of security as possible. At the least the first few points that will be mentioned.

In reality you may only be able to apply some of the measures for securing the principal. This is due to the operational environment, which does not really allow for covert teams (they won't blend in) to be inserted and sniper teams due to the danger factor. Some of the functions such as surveillance won't be applied due to the budgetary constraints, the danger factor, and using locals won't be practical as they won't have the training.

Some teams may have PSD operators that can do a number of different roles inside the team and at times function in one capacity on one operation and then in a different capacity on another operation within the same team.

One of the functions could be the driver who could also be the team medic. The combat vehicle which normally have all the best shooters and combat experienced operators might have operators that can do the counter sniper role as well.

Operators with a lot of knowledge when it comes to explosives might do the function of IED search on vehicles and if qualified for EOD to do this function as well. Most team members should have at least good weapons abilities, medical training and as some of the operators will be from a SF unit, they will have a good cross section of training that will benefit the team as a whole.

If an operator has 3 major skills, then he has much more chance of being useful in a PSD operation than most. These could be as an example level 5 or more medical, EOD qualified, sniper qualified and surveillance qualified. Most SF operators should have some of these as it's a prerequisite of being an operator.

PSD operation team elements

The size and composition of the team depends on the **budget**, the specific **type of operation** and who the **client is (government, business person)**. Even though we discuss all the areas that can be applied in a PSD situation it will only be practical to apply some of the teams to the security in your operational environment due to the constraints discussed before. It will be up to the leadership to decide which aspects of PSD operations they want to apply and which do not need to be applied in their area of operations.

Each company will differ in leadership organization, so the number of team leaders (TL) will change for each company.

Team Leader

There will be a number of team leaders. These will be the overall team leader that coordinates all convoys and overseas residence security handles intel and liaises with the person in charge of the PSD Company.

1. Convoy team leader who has control of the whole convoy
2. Specific TL's such as combat car commander or QRF team leader if the company has one.
3. Training team leader (coordinates all training)

Escort Section

- Escort section of the PSD convoy: they perform the foot escort function as well.
- TL of the vehicle and foot escort: his responsibility is to control the principal and direct the team and will normally be the most experienced person in the team.
- Drivers, must have the advanced driving skills to function in a PSD team this includes driving heavy armored vehicles
- The PSD operators, they will perform the foot escort and deal with any attack enroute as well as secure the perimeter when stationary

Undercover operators

In an environment where these are practical, they should be applied. The undercover operators are not strictly part of the escort as they don't walk with the principal, but are an essential part of the team when this function is needed. One of the reasons undercover teams are not used in the Iraq and Afghanistan areas is because the operators would not be able to blend in to the environment.

Drivers

Drivers normally do all the driving but these might be chosen from the teams and rotated to different position in the team if they are not dedicated drivers, which they should be to get the most secure situation.

Most convoys will constitute 3 vehicles which will be the

1. The point vehicle (in front) (their call sign can be Victor 1)
2. The VIP vehicle (middle, don't always put the principal in this vehicle, unless you don't like him!) (Victor 2)
3. The combat vehicle at the back (Victor 3)

Driver types:

1. **Drivers:** normally do all the driving but these might be chosen from the teams (PSD operators) and rotated to different position in the team if they are not dedicated drivers.
2. **Driver TL:** The drivers may have a person specifically designated to teach and ensure driving standards. He won't be the convoy team leader as his job is to ensure driving standards.
3. **PSD drivers:** Drivers that understand how to handle a vehicle that is 4.5-6 tons instead of a normal SUV that weighs 2.5 tons.

Combat operators

Operators that deal with combat aspects of an attack.

79

HQ personnel

1. they do the coordinating of all aspects of the team movement
2. recording of daily team functions such as where the convoy is and liaison
3. Take SITREPs from outlaying bases if the company has them.
4. Sometimes the post and equipment arrivals will be taken in by the HQ personnel and recorded.
5. Radio operators
6. Tracking personnel (use the tracking software that tracks PSD escort)
7. Liaison with military and PSD which is sometimes done by overall TL.
8. The overall TL will also normally work from this location.

Advance team

Advance team is not normally a function in a war zone as any prior check by (expat) personnel will alert the insurgents. So if you want to do an advance function the people will have to blend in.

1. Advance team leader
2. Operators
3. Optional in a large company
   a. EOD
   b. Counter sniper
   c. Covert operators

Residence security

Residence security (sometimes done by locals). It is expedient that an ex-pat is in charge of this area of security.

TL is normally a PSD operator (it helps if the person speaks the local language).

Perimeter security Team is normally locals.

Counter sniper

Counter sniper (only for large companies with the manpower and clients to warrant this). Counter snipers are inserted hours or even in some cases days before and are also not part of the actual escort but in some situations are a valuable asset in certain situations. These are the elements of the sniper team:

1. **Sniper**: uses a 7.62 x 51 caliber semi-auto weapon with a 4-10 x 50 reticule scopes. Best weapons would be FN, H7K G3, M14, Galil in 7.62x51.
2. **Spotter**: gives the sniper targets and covers him to the front, his weapon could be a 5.56x 45 caliber with a Trijicon scope.
3. **Security**: should have a high-capacity weapon with the ability to engage targets fast and reliably.

Explosive ordinance disposal (EOD)

EOD is normally not the responsibility of the company but of military in country, if the company has the resources and clients to warrant this type of personnel then it would be a consideration for regions where the military presence is sparse.

Surveillance detection

The counter surveillance team will normally only be for government type contracts where the manpower and logistics are available. This is where the surveillance done by the terrorists is detected and then surveillance done on the terrorists by the team if the budget and manpower is available. This is also only viable with a large team as it is very time consuming and expensive to do surveillance.

Counter surveillance would not normally be applicable to a war zone as the PSD operators won't fit into the environment. These guys do the surveillance on the terrorist surveillance.

Logistics coordinator

This person's job is to ensure all equipment such as weapons, food, ammo, water, optics, maps, vehicles etc. arrive at the PSD HQ on time and are taken to the appropriate places. This may be sleeping quarters outside of the PSD operations compound. It may also be that the company has smaller bases outside of town which will need supplies.

General expediencies for high threat contracts

1. Have a comprehensive medical kit in the vehicles available for emergencies.
2. Ensure that the vehicles are in perfect working order, engine, tires etc.
3. Know your enemies, learn all you can about their tactics and methods.
4. Have at least 2 to 3 means of communications to base and medical evacuation. Radios UHF, VHF base sets and hand held, cell phones, satellite phones, FM hand held radios.
5. Maintain your condition; focus on short sprints and endurance walks. **Keep hydrated** as this decreases performance as you get dehydrated, and **stretching** will stop you getting stiff.
6. Regularly check batteries and equipment **not used** to see if it still functioning.
7. Practice contact drills as a team at least 1 to 2 times per week, even if it is dry runs for 2 to 3 hours per session.

General Strategies for Countering PSD Threats

The main types of threats are:

1. Ambushes
2. Improvised explosive devices
3. Suicide bombers
4. Kidnapping
5. Sniper

Attacks and ambushes can be initiated by any type of weapon such as an IED, sniper weapon or even just a road block, they then will proceed with assault rifles to finish the job once your convoy has been stopped. Normally in countries such as Iraq and Afghanistan they use IED's to initiate the attack then assault rifles and grenades to finish. They can happen in many different combinations with the weapons mentioned above. The difference between attacks and ambushes and specific IED attacks is that the IED placed on its own with no further attacks is just that and IED. Ambushes are initiated and then continued with other weapons. This could be to get hostages or to finish the people being attacked.

These skills and strategies will help against all types of attacks:

Observation and awareness

1. It starts when you leave the compound but you also need to be aware in the event of abduction, which can take place anywhere.
2. Awareness is a state of mind and not a physical skill even though you do use your eyes, ears, smell and anticipation in your awareness.
3. Practice your scanning till it becomes second nature. Part of these skills are the method of scanning close (crowds)and far (windows, doors) as well as your mental such as OAP (observe anticipate and plan)

Individual skills, especially combat skills

This includes all forms of combat but specifically includes

1. Movement ability in combat whether unarmed or with weapons
2. Fitness
3. Rifle
4. Handgun
5. Blade
6. Unarmed (all Close Protection operators should be well versed in close quarter fighting)

Minimize the principal's exposure

1. Don't go where there is a **high** danger of being attacked
2. Move from the vehicle to a venue quickly and smoothly
3. Don't drive if you don't have to, sometimes failed operators were just in the wrong place at the wrong time.
4. Be prepared with all the correct equipment and tactics for the specific operation (e.g., open country=sniper system, night driving= NV, crowds=undercover operator)
5. Have the right equipment for the job.
6. Be low profile where possible (don't drive in a vehicle that gives you away)
7. Take special care at areas of heightened danger (crowds, open roads travelled by security forces, known terrorist hot spots).

Strategies for countering ambushes

How you counter different types of threats will vary. You should have skills that count for all types of threats, such as awareness. Ambushes have to be reasonably manpower intensive and therefore make it easier to spot them than a hidden /camouflaged IED. The kidnapping threat is also difficult to spot as most times when deception is used you won't realize it till very late in the attack, this is where knowing the MO of the groups in the area of operations help. The sniper threat is more easily defended against by applying preventative methods as it is extremely difficult to spot a well camouflaged sniper. Even if the sniper is not camouflaged it is still difficult to see as they can be placed hundreds of meters away from you in the operational environment.

Countering ambushes once they have begun by using good counter attack tactics:

- These are discussed in vehicle anti-ambush drills later in this manual.
- Foot anti ambush drills

Know your enemy and their capabilities.

Strategies for IED's

Countering IED's is by understanding how they are deployed. Later in this manual there'll be more information on IED identification.

1. Types (C4, 80mm mortar, canon shells, anti-tank mines)
2. Ways getting to target: by foot, donkey/horse cart, vehicle

Where they are placed

1. Pot holes in ground
2. Ballard (side of the road)
3. Carcass of any animal big enough
4. Vehicle's VBIED's
5. Side walk: built into the cement
6. Coke can, bottles, teddy bear etc.
7. Narrow sections of the road (between hills, bridges)
8. Where the road makes a bend
9. Flyovers (while you are below or on top)

How they are camouflaged

1. Built into side walk by using plaster of Paris mold
2. Put in carcass of donkey, dog, sheep etc.
3. Disguised as everyday items such as coke can (small IED)
4. Placed in Ballard at head height (normally shaped charge that shoots copper disc sideways)
5. Placed near or in rubbish bag
6. Placed in old IED craters

How they are triggered

1. Cell phone

2. Garage door opener
3. Infra-red
4. Command (wire from terrorist to the IED)
5. Booby traps (initiated by the person)
    a. Pressure release
    b. Pressure
    c. Tilt (mercury)

Once you know the way the threat is made, deployed, concealed and activated then you can develop ways of fighting against it.

Background information on IED's

Later in this manual we'll look at IED's in more detail with examples of different types.

IED's have been used in many terrorist operations since the 1950's and they continue to be used and adapted to the theatre where they are employed such as Afghanistan, Iraq, Spain (Basque), Ireland (IRA), Russia (Chechens), US, South Africa (Pagad) etc. It is the main concern for PSD operators because of the **increased sophistication** in the initial stages of the war the IED's were basic devices that were not always placed in such a way that made them effective. With time the devices have increased in size such as truck VBIED as seen in footage on YouTube. Then you have increased sophistication types such as the type used such as the shaped charges used from about 2005/6 onwards and the latest is the use of small shaped charge thrown with a parachute to disable the vehicle as it hits the engine. In the early stages of the insurgency in Iraq the IED's were very basic with the focus on concealment (roadside pavement, carcasses, in the tar of the road, in old holes made by previous IED's).

The new focus is on shaped charges. This skill was learned from outside the borders more than likely from intelligence services of a country like Pakistan or Turkey. These are as their name suggests shaped charges, so they propel hot copper through the armor of vehicle's sides as the vehicle passes a bridge which sometimes has sand filled containers used as protection for check point bollards etc. Lately, approximately 2008, we see the introduction of hand-held projectiles that are thrown by hand on top of the vehicle's bonnet to detonate downwards. It is thrown as the convoy passes and incapacitates the vehicle which is a perfect time for an assault by insurgents. You should then expect an attack from another place by insurgents using rifles as this is sometimes a type of holding or delaying strategy.

The ease of use makes it the safest method to use for insurgents when attacking a convoy.

IED effects on PSD vehicle operations

1. Means of deployment of IED's (improvised explosive devices) and VBIED's (Vehicle borne improvised explosive device)
   a. Concealed (carcass, rubbish bags, smaller ones in cool drink cans)
   b. Disguised (VBIED, suicide bombers hard to stop)
   c. Deception (distracting the convoy to move to the other side of the road where the IED really is)
   d. Fake IED to assess your response
2. Size and effectiveness of IED and VBIED's
   a. Briefcase/pipe bomb (see notes on evacuation distance)
   b. Self-manufactured explosives (can be almost any size)
   c. Bombs (80mm mortar)
   d. Old or stolen land mines
   e. Canon shells
   f. Sedan VBIED
   g. Truck VBIED (these are the most powerful as seen in footage)
3. PSD vulnerabilities
   a. Predictability (of where you leave, when you leave where you go etc.)
   b. Limited armor capabilities for transport (normally the best armor will be level 7)
   c. Limited manpower (small teams)
   d. Limited firepower (normally only assault rifles allowed?)
   e. Training not suitable to urban operations
   f. Limited backup (limited to private companies size and structure). Military has fewer restrictions due to

       their size.

   g. Large hostile population

   h. From years of fighting sophisticated attacks

4. Overcoming these vulnerabilities

   a. Drive as many **different routes** at different **times** with as many **variations** of your convoy tactics and configuration of where the principal goes (position in the convoy) as possible

   b. **Use military type armored** if in your budget (it might be overt but they are even used by the US) vehicle from SA if possible, these are the V shaped anti mine vehicles designed for the border war.

   c. limit travel where possible

   d. Go covert at times

   e. Fly when possible (this is possible if you know the local military commander). Some PSD teams had this as a benefit

   f. Move in as **big a team** as possible.

   g. Use the weapons with the max amount of firepower such belt fed LMG or **high-capacity magazines** such as C-mag and 75 round drum mags for the AK and PKM.

   h. Make sure you also have **precision weapons** for the long-distance standoff situations. Precision weapon should preferably be 7.62x51 cal. With a 4 to 10 magnification scope.

   i. **Be creative** disguise and change (times, forms of transport mode of transport armored vehicle to taxi as an example), disinformation, let their agents hear you are to leave at a specific time and leave later, this only works if there are people that will hear and take the info to the right ears. This could be one of the cleaners, maid, chef as these will be in a good place to eves drop on your principal

j. Make arrangements with other companies and military where possible to support you and assist you and let them know you will reciprocate. **Share QRF responsibilities** if possible and if it's within your capabilities. **Share training** ideas and help each other and in this way you will build a healthy relationship with other operators.

k. **Share intel with others and they will be more likely to help you.** Build up your network where you can this can militarily contacts, as well as locals and PSD operators

l. **Have your own QRF** (quick reaction force) or rapid response team available to support any operators caught in a situation. Transport should be a **helicopter or military type armored vehicles South African type if possible (these were used with great success)** if possible and team should be 4 to 8 properly equipped operators. More would be better but it might not be possible to have 8 operators sitting waiting for action unless you were the size of Black Water.

The means by which the IED's are triggered by the terrorists are also varied and depend on the training and influence by **other groups**, who may be involved in the training of the local terrorist.

Their method of operation that is the terrorist way of using IED's is affected by who trained them, whether it's the CIA, Turkey, Iran etc.

Countering suicide bombers

Suicide bomber overview

Definition: Operational method in which the very definition of the attack is, dependent upon the death of the perpetrator.

Advantages for the terrorists for this method (suicide attacker) of attack:

1. Perpetrator chooses the time and place
2. Simpler to plan as you do not need escape as part of the planning
3. Cheaper
4. No or very little danger of capture, unless the device does not work or the person loses heart.
5. Huge impact on the population of the targeted area.
6. Good publicity for group carrying it out (if you can call it good).

From studies we can say the following:

All studies will show trends at a particular time and at a particular geographical area, so these trends can change depending on the emphasis placed by the people doing the indoctrination.

1. The suicide terrorist will normally be younger in comparing to a non-suicide terrorist. The most affected age group being 22-27 years of age.
2. They will normally be unmarried
3. They will normally be more religious, have more study in religion and ideology
4. Depending on the region and period most suicide, bombers are men. Only 3-4% being woman.

Statistics for period 1993-2002 complied from 80 suicide and 663 non-suicide attacks over that period. These stats apply mainly to Israel

1. Of a total of 743 attacks
2. 23% were car bombs
3. 77% were carried on the body

Suicide bomber targets

1. 9% against non-urban targets
2. 23% against buses and railway stations
3. 30% against public transportation
4. 38% Shopping centers

This will change when it comes to a war zone such as Iraq and Afghanistan because it is easier to get a vehicle close to the military forces of the coalition than it is to walk up and the affect is very different because you can only carry so much explosive before it becomes obvious and this will allow the security forces to recognize the attack.

Know the signs/signals

The problem is that other factors can cause some of the signs making it very difficult in the hustle and bustle of traffic to discern this.

1. Age of the attacker, be aware that in some regions this will change but for Israel; this was 20 to 30 years of age
2. Type of target they will hit (discussed above)
3. Signs of tension clenched fist, sweating, nerves disposition.
4. Fixated on the target (if you are aware of this then it is easier to pick up)
5. The adrenaline will cause the person to have a less fluid gate and a more robotic walk because the adrenaline reduces the fine motor function.
6. The pupils will dilate when the adrenaline flows but then it's too late if you see this. This is easier to see with blued eyed persons than dark eyed people.

Know the methods and procedure

1. Carried by a person (dress/ demeanor)
2. Speed and determination: they approach with the fixation shows on the face and this comes across as determination
3. The person will look overweight for their features they will have less fat on the face compared to their girth.
4. They will be weighed down by the weight of the explosives; this will increase exertion, sweating and girth of the person.

Keep them away from the foot escort

1. Keep your distance from following persons or anybody in the area and start to plan (OAP) if you see a person approach that has no reason to. This is very difficult in an uncontrolled crowd as some gatherings will be,
2. So if possible, have security to control the crowd and keep them at a safe distance.
3. Look for people coming out of the crowd faster than the rest, this is easier if the people are standing still.
4. Sometimes only one person will approach you from the crowd you can warn them and engage as needed sometimes this follows in quick succession. Everybody worldwide understands the language of a rifle pointed at them so if they don't stop shoot in PSD (very high Threat situations). This is not a good situation to be in so suggest to the principal that you stay away from crowds, no crowded areas very few problems.
5. This becomes very difficult if not impossible in a crowd to **try to avoid crowds. (in case you did not get it the first time)**

Important Scenarios can include this type of an attack

Countering VBIED's

VBIED's overview

There are a few things which make the VBIED more attractive to the insurgents /terrorists in a war zone

1. You can carry more explosives, which has more effect against armored vehicles military and civilian contractors.
2. It gets to the target faster and less likely to attract attention
3. It can be left alongside the road for passing mil or contractors
4. It can be driven then left by anybody to the target area.
5. It is easier to disguise the vehicle for example an ambulance, mil vehicle, taxi, bus goods truck etc.

Know the signs/signals

The problem is that other factors can cause some of the signs making it very difficult in the hustle and bustle of traffic to discern this.

1. Age of the attacker
2. Type of target they will hit (discussed above)
3. Signs of tension
4. Fixated on the target (if you are aware of this then it is easier to pick up)
5. The face may have a deadpan look as the person anticipates the result but this will be difficult to tell from a distance.

Know the methods and procedure

1. Carried by a person (dress/ demeanor)
2. For VBIED's how the vehicle approaches occupants age of occupants give you an indicator (discussed in doc)
3. Speed and determination they approach with
4. Vehicle might look weighted down due to weight of the explosives

Keep them away from the convoy

1. Keep your distance from following vehicles
2. Look for the vehicles coming out of the crowd faster than the rest
3. Sometimes only one stupid half-asleep person will try to get past the rest, wave them down then warn then engage sometimes this follows in quick succession

Shockwave from truck VBIED:

Hit on a Humvee initial explosion on left with just dust afterwards right

LiveLeak

LiveLeak

Sniper Threats

Reports on sniper attacks on US troops in Iraq give you an idea of the threat posed by snipers:

- Snipers use the dense city environment to their advantage. When a US patrol comes under fire, the sniper could be shooting from hundreds of possible vantage points.
- US troops often can't return fire for fear of hitting civilians and angering locals.
- Urban operations give snipers many possible targets.
- Intel on insurgents shows them gathering manuals and videos on sniping techniques. These in turn show snipers are trained to prioritize targeting medics, engineers, and chaplains. These targets are designed to demoralize Western forces.
- Some snipers use a hole in the trunk of a vehicle to shoot from.

Question: what caliber weapon is this weapon in the picture above and its effective range?

When making an assessment of the area for PSD operations for possible sniper activity, when doing a threat analysis, you should consider the issues herein.

Collect the information and get hold of a map of the area and work out the most likely areas the sniper will shoot from. Always have an experienced sniper to help and tell you where the most likely spots would be that he would use and to help in assessing the area. The area does not have to be specific – it can be an area of a couple of meters across if it is a bushy area, a couple of rocks, a hill with cover (hollow in the ground).

Previous sniper activity

1. If no previous sniper activity, then this just means you won't
   be expecting it when it happens. Never go on previous
   experience when considering the principal's safety, it just
   means you plan as if there were the threats you know about
   but it is unlikely you will get sniped any time soon.
2. If there was previous activity of sniping then you can work on
   counters for the MO, which will always be limited because of
   the nature of an individual and their specific character traits.
3. How many snipers were active and do you know their
   procedures and how they carry out their operations?
4. There will be preferred positions in an area. Know what these
   would be in the event you get shot at and need to locate the
   sniper during an event or attack.

Previous sniper activity method of operations (MO)

1. How did they get to the target area?
2. How did they conceal themselves, darkened room, roof top, bushes, vehicle etc.?
3. Did they use high ground or a hide (bushes, trees etc.)?

Sniper limitations

1. Caliber used (you will know when you find the bullet). This will give you an idea of the weapon's maximum range.
2. **Range** shot at when **missed** and range shot at when **hit** the target (skill level).
3. What is the maximum range or capacity of the caliber used?

Question: what caliber weapon is this weapon in the picture above and its effective range?

Sniper performance over time

When a sniper has been active for a while, he will either get better or he will get sloppy depending on his character.

1. If the sniper has been going for a while you should have an idea of how he functions. This will help you if you have to search an area quickly for the sniper when he fires.
2. If he gets sloppy, you will have a better chance at catching him.
3. If you want to bait a sniper, never do so with a live person – use some form of dummy such as a helmet, mannequin, be creative (not that you would find one in the places you will find yourself) to draw the person out it is not worth a soldier's life to catch one sniper.

Sniper timelines

What time of the day do the snipers operate?

1. Any sniper working an area has to get in and out – what is the logical path in and out of the area?
2. The sniper can leave just by making a hit if the concealment is easy to reach such as in a building.
3. Hides in a bush need to be occupied before a people get up in the morning so a person is not alerted.

Sniper preferred targets

Which personnel do the snipers aim/ shoot for?

1. Officers
2. Medics
3. Engineers
4. PSD
5. LMG gunners
6. Other, as in any personal following the military team as in reporters
7. Diplomats (as in Iraq)
8. Bomb disposal
9. Infantry on patrol

Counter strategies for sniper activity

The information gathered from the above assessment will help you to minimize the threat to you and the principle as the PSD team will also be a target of opportunity to any sniper.

Immediate action drills

1. **Get yourself and principal to solid cover** not over looked by a high point if possible. Don't stick your head out and if you do search then use binoculars where possible. This must be done from a **concealed** spot where possible. Inside a bushy area can be reasonable **concealment** not **cover**.
2. If you are in the open **keep moving** and give covering fire while on the move, especially if you have an idea of where the sniper is, which is unlikely as they will go to great lengths to conceal their position.
3. Use **probing fire** if the terrain allows (open bushy area, hostile area where little or no **non**combatants). This is focused firing at possible positions.
4. If you need to move and the situation allows then give **covering fire.** This is nonspecific firing, it can be referred to as covering fire or suppressing fire to keep the sniper's head down. This will only work if it is close enough to be a threat to the sniper.
5. If you feel you can approach a sniper's position without being shot do so quickly, just remember a good sniper would have thought of this and you may get shot if you leave cover without some covering fire or smoke to disguise your movement.
6. If you can play the sound back in your head, and try to imagine the sound and how long it was between the crack and the bang this will give you and approximate range. **Look for cover at that range, do this from a concealed position.**

Vehicle convey planning considerations

1. Previous sniper activity and MO of the sniper
2. Limitations of the individual sniper's maximum effective range
3. Possible cover in the event of an attack
4. Closest place to the entrance you can stop with vehicle of your venue you are going to visit
5. How to position the vehicles to give maximum cover.

Abductions

Abduction are carried out with less frequency than IED attacks and ambushes but they are normally well planned and well executed.

The target will be selected for the following reasons:

1. The media value of the target, the amount of exposure they get from the event. This will depend on the abductors' goals.
2. The ease with which the abduction can be executed.
3. The target selection and surveillance may happen at the same time to be able to select the correct target once the information has been collected.

The surveillance may be done as a final surveillance or as a group, surveillance where a number of targets are chosen to collect as much on the target as possible, or a little on each target to choose the correct one.

Abduction chain of events

1. Target selection, possible targets are nominated
2. Initial surveillance of a couple of possible targets
3. Final target selection
4. Target selection may revolve around testing the protection team's response by faking e.g., swerving their vehicle in front of you.
5. Surveillance and planning, where, how and when to attack
6. Dummy runs, rehearsals (testing the team, swerving in front of the vehicle etc.)
7. Allocation and selection of attack element
8. Attack
9. Removal of the target to a venue if taken hostage
10. Holding and propaganda

The above progression may not be as complex as shown above if the terrorist group does not have the resources and time to do a thorough surveillance. It may be a target selection a few days or weeks of surveillance then the abduction. This would be unusual though because most abduction are planned and executed with good precision.

Abduction techniques

The techniques can be as varied as you want them to be. The common ones will be dealt with:

1. **Checkpoint** deception: this is done by obtaining Iraqi police uniforms or US army uniforms and masquerading as one of these forces. They then use a checkpoint or stop the convoy pretending to be Iraqi police they then deal with the security team and proceed to take the principal. Another deception can be to masquerade as US forces and then take the principal hostage.
2. **Deceptive invitation/directions**. Another way is to deceive the target (say a journalist, contractor, soldier) into going to an area where they can be apprehended by a criminal cell who will then hand them to a terrorist group for $10 000. This deception will almost always be by a local who knows the value of a foreigner.
3. **Ambush**: where they see where the convoy is most vulnerable to attack and then set it up and attempt to kill the security or kidnap them if they can. They then try to take the principal hostage and take him to a safehouse they have chosen beforehand.

Countering abduction attacks

Abductors can strike in a variety of ways so there's no specific counter measure. You need fundamentally sound close protection procedures using the techniques covered in this manual and my CP manual, as well as the weapons manuals.

Situational Awareness

Awareness is the ability to observe the environment around you and calculate or determine to an extent what is going on and how it will affect you as an individual or a team, and then act on that information correctly to overcome the problem that presents itself. In self-defense this could be seeing a group of possible attackers then making a plan and acting on it. In a military context it could be noticing an ambush or indications of an ambush such as enemy equipment (footprints, camp fire smell) and then taking the appropriate action to nullify the ambush or break through it and so on.

This is the very beginning of any type of self-defense or military function where you work in a small or large team. This is because understanding the position of where the enemy is compared to your position is very important to succeeding in combat. This and understanding the enemy's disposition with regards to weapons training and equipment etc.

You can have all the training in the world but that cannot help you if you are not aware of your surroundings. "In the street" it's mostly about the criminal element. In a military situation it's about a lot more than just the enemy it's about terrain your enemy's capability your personal situation (readiness) friendlies and enemy assets etc.

Area awareness:

1. Immediate area awareness is essential to combat survival, personal survival (self-defense) and other areas such as escape and evasion. This is so that you know which direction your enemy is, and how close they are will dictate how and what you use to defend yourself with.
2. Extended area awareness is essential for planning immediate actions and preparation, you need extended awareness for temporary bases, hold up points and so on. This is normally

done with OP/LP (listening post or observation post) but can also be done with binocular (terrain allowing)/ monocular /spotting scope. Another way of achieving wider areas awareness is the drone, which can do a 360 degree around your LP/OP or temporary base.

Long term awareness of potential scenarios with regards to the enemy disposition and intentions will also play a major role, but we are mainly concerned with situational awareness here as to your combat environment. This being the immediate danger to you and therefore the situation as it unfolds around you at the point in time.

Every person in your team, that means <u>every single person,</u> is an intelligence gatherer and creates your situational awareness. This is done by constantly feeding information to each other as you move through the terrain.

Increasing situational awareness **using technology** such as:

1. Small drone
2. Night Vision (NV) technology (scope or monocular)
3. Thermal scope or monocular
4. Possibly a range finder to estimate or know fairly accurately how far the enemy is with regards to your position.
5. More crudely you could use nylon tied as 'trip wire' to a soda can with pebbles in that shake as a person disturbs the can if they walk into the nylon. The nylon could run through/ around your area and the can be inside your hide so as to only alert you.

Awareness is only **valuable if** it is **coupled with calculation** (planning) and the correct actions such as a correct attack aggressive counter ambush (attacking an ambush) or tactical withdrawal (moving away with covering fire) or attack and withdrawal. It could also mean just staying still to allow the enemy to pass, especially in a 'reconnaissance' purpose or objective in the context of a listening post in a war zone (non-permissive environment), or in the context of "the street" negating a possible mugging by taking another route to bypass a possible criminal party. So awareness is essential in a combat environment including self-defense in the street.

OAP = awareness (i.e., consider "observe anticipate plan" as being an acronym for "awareness"). This gives you a way of dealing with your environment:

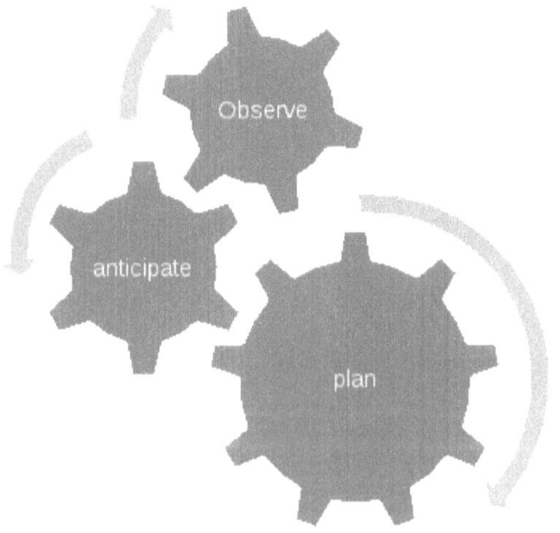

There are **<u>no varying levels or degrees of awareness</u>** – you are either ***aware or not***. Once you are aware, this then leads to observing the attacker and deciding what you will do (this is the planning phase of OAP) this then changes to a combat mindset, which is a cold aggression. To say there are levels of awareness means you know when trouble is about to strike and also that there are times when you don't have to be fully aware. Common sense tells you that awareness is a mindset that should always be present while you are awake and that you only relax when you are asleep. Think of it as a sense of awareness yet with a relaxed disposition (character) of the body and this will become second nature to you.

It is not a tense and furtive disposition, but a relaxed and calm awareness (cognizance); you take in the environmental stimulus and calculate the possibilities of how the world might change around you. A relaxed disposition and demeanor allow the mind to flirt over the myriad of possibilities this might even be subconscious in some aspects and this is called your sixth sense which is made keener through experience.

Aspects of awareness

Awareness is a continual process of looking and calculating what is happening in your immediate environment. Awareness is the mental process of looking and then asking yourself questions e.g., why a person is standing or sitting in a specific place. Do they pay unnecessary attention to you and do they mimic your movements? Did they move off as you moved past them – this could be coincidence or planned? Once your awareness has become second nature and you don't have to consciously look around then it has become part of your everyday functions.

Awareness starts a decision-making process. Self-defense will most likely apply to areas that are built up such as towns because they are where you will most likely find various criminal elements this will be due to abundance of targets for such criminals.

A questioning mindset is a calculating mind calculating leads to assessment and this leads to planning and the quality of plan will be dictated by your experience and quality of your training. *The following example questions to ask yourself when observing your environment apply more to a self-defense/combat situation:*

1. Is it normal for a person to stand in a particular location where you've observed someone?
2. Why are those 3 people looking around nervously, possibly communicating with each other?
3. Why are those guys communicating surreptitiously over the road to each other by looking around and then at each other?
4. Should that person be dressed so warmly in such a hot climate?
5. Did they follow me as I passed by and then turn when I turned?
6. Why are those individuals just standing around, with no

obvious purpose?

Awareness issues for SHTF conflict

Questions concerning awareness for SHTF conflict will be slightly different; here it could be in the countryside or towns:

- Depending on the terrain your questions might address 'sign' left by people moving through your area of operations such as spoor (footprints). Here you would want to know how many people there were, their direction of travel, signs of weapons (equipment left behind or imprint of stock where person leant weapon against a tree), fires, broken branches from moving through, grass trampled down, etc.
- Open terrain, such as we would find in farm land or bushveld, would mean looking for observation points people might take for OP/LP, farm houses any man-made structure camp sites (in SHTF they might be a danger but in normal situation they won't). It will be similar to your military operations because of the terrain the difference is in a civil unrest situation (SHTF) even civilians might be potential enemies.
- Because of the lack of crowds, it would be much more obvious if there were people in the area and they would stand out and anybody in the area would attract your attention. You would ask yourself what their purpose was and a period of approximately 1 hour will give you some indication of what they are doing in the area. That is if you have time to observe them as your objective might be purely a distraction which means it would be irrelevant unless you are looking for some equipment that they might have or food or water.
- Another aspect of traveling in open (rural) environments would be looking for shelter/cover when you need to stop and rest. Depending on the type of situation security

considerations will be relevant especially in a SHTF type scenario. The shelter would preferably be close to water and have a high point to look over the land from as well as avenues of escape.

- Questions that might come to mind in a combat environment when occupying your shelter and when observing the movement of potential combatants will be if they are tracking you or just happen to be in the area. Either way your pack should be packed or ready to go, so don't unpack until you are sure you are in a fairly safe area. Only take out what you need at that time e.g., food and water.

- Open terrain has more potential for an all-out attack by a party as in an urban environment where they have to potentially contend with the police or other bystanders. This will be negated by the fact that you will most probably be moving with a long gun in semi auto.

Key points in awareness

1. *Question how people are acting in relation to their environment and to you.* Normally potentially hostile individuals would be moving quickly (or quicker than the rest of the public) if in a following (tracking) context and they would be looking around for witnesses. They might also possibly reaching for something in their pockets; this can also be checking to reassure themselves e.g., that their knife/gun is still there. This could also be looking at someone to communicate or reassure themselves. Such signs could be the precursor to an attack or a possible intention to attack, whether it is carried through or not.

2. *Study the body language of people.* This might differ slightly for different cultures but the base stuff still stays the same. Some cultures are more excitable and use their hands more, for example the Italians are more volatile and expressive. Arabic culture is also more excitable than western cultures as is Israeli which is the cousin of the Arab you could quite easily think there was a major argument going on in a street in Jerusalem. This might be a minor disagreement or even just casual conversation. Keep this in mind. The Germans are more subdued and calmer; if you saw Germans acting like Italians then you would be alarmed. General body language signs of tension examples are: are their **shoulders hunched or fist clenched** or are their **hands holding something which could be a weapon** and generally being furtive (eyes moving faster than normal) with **eyes move side to side (this might not be obvious but observable)?** These signs could be the precursor to an attack. You will have to be close to see many additional signs e.g., pupil dilatation in the eyes could be from adrenaline or drugs – either way that could mean

danger to you. Keep in mind people who are up to something no good will have a certain tension about them that is visible if you know what to look for.

3. **Use your *peripheral vision*** at all times, especially while walking or moving through buildings and doors. This helps to pick up a person approaching from the side, especially quick movement should be quite apparent to your peripheral vision. Looking backwards and using your peripheral vision you can detect quick movement. This is a very valuable tool for scanning 360 degrees around you and should become part of your everyday habits.

4. When walking, turning your head and using your peripheral vision allows you to see behind you if someone is following or moving in quickly to close the gap between you and them. They will be more visible to you because they are moving faster than the surrounding foot traffic. **See diagram below** for the "360-degree scan" technique.

5. Looking ***close*** and ***far*** helps to control an area more effectively with visual observation. Close can be doorways and such, and far can be vehicles in the distance, bushes, trees, parks (places where criminals can hang out without being disturbed). Be especially aware when leaving your vehicle/home arriving back at your vehicle/home, and going in/out of a shop/restaurant or similar venue.

6. Looking ***slightly down*** when surrounded gives you a better view of who is around you and where they are placed (this is if they are standing fairly close to you 1-5 meters). You would not be standing around if they were armed with weapons such as handguns and rifles as this would be a death sentence, you need to shoot and or move fast while shooting or just moving fast, shooting and moving is far superior because of the shock factor that causes the enemy to miss and run.

7. Remember, **do not ignore that feeling you get about a situation (sixth sense)**, but can't explain what it is, a feeling that the situation 'is not right'. Don't ignore it because this is a capability God gave you to asses a situation *subconsciously* to protect you from danger. Don't listen to nonsense about how such techniques evolved over trillions of years – leave fantasy for children's books. It's part of your programming by the Master builder and programmer, Himself.

Exercise to train awareness

1. This should be done at a low intensity to avoid injury
2. It is a **mental exercise** and not an intensity exercise
3. This will increase your decision-making process and tactics
4. It will allow you to use your peripheral vision more efficiently

Stand with 3 or 4 people (potential assailants) around the student and each such person can have a different type of training weapon (e.g., plastic knife or handgun). Such weapons could include a handgun knife or baton such as an impact weapon; and something non-lethal such as a cell phone. The idea is to force you to make quick decisions as to which person to engage. This is a mental process so you can even use your fingers to point at the person who you think is the most dangerous to you and which one you would engage in order of importance as to which attacker poses the greatest threat. It is also an awareness process so watching as many of the individuals as possible is part of the exercise and this should help with awareness in general.

1. *This is more important than you think so don't ignore this exercise.*
2. Attackers can initially only present their weapons and the student must decide which person he/she would neutralize first. They could even use a finger just to point at the opponent, because it's a mental exercise not a shooting one.
3. Then extend the drill by allowing the surrounding people to move towards the student slowly as this will also force the student to decide which the priority person to stop first is and which weapon is more dangerous at which range.

The "360° scan" technique

The following diagram illustrates what is meant earlier above about using your peripheral vision. Here NV stand for normal vision and PV stands for peripheral vision. In the diagram below we have a view from the top of how you turn your head and use your peripheral vision to scan the area behind you, to front and sides.

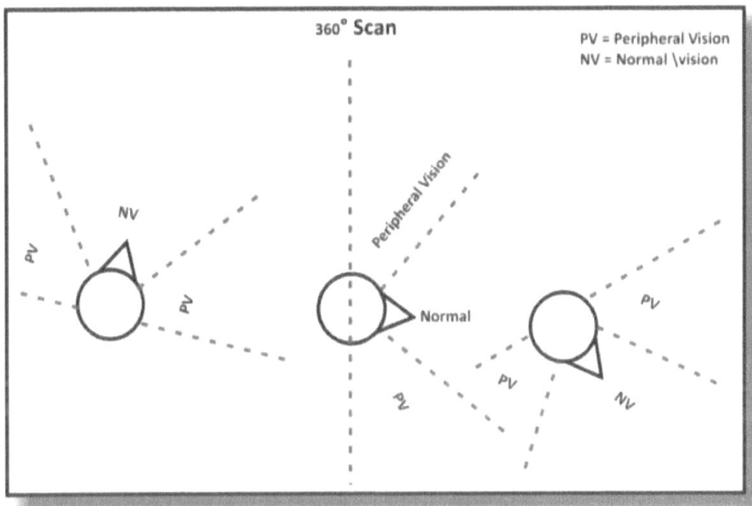

An example of awareness in action

Imagine you are looking around in an urban setting and notice a guy standing doing nothing just watching everybody (trying to act casual) with his shoulders hunched and he's looking slightly tense. This scenario could happen many times as you are walking around during the day or night. Your observation becomes a casual way of assessing your environment.

You decide to access your blade *covertly* as you walk past or up an alley. You realize the person followed you so you turn keeping the blade away from the attacker so they can't see it or grab your arm to try to disarm you or stop you using your hand with the blade in it.

The attacker lunges for your briefcase and you deflect the attack and proceed to *incapacitate* the attacker with your weapon. Keep in mind this could mean going from fist to blade and then to pistol. Depending on what you instinctively feel is appropriate for the context this will always be your choice and should be encouraged by the instructor. This is to give you the confidence and ability to deal with a combat situation.

You assess the situation once you have incapacitated your attacker and observe your surroundings to see if there are any more attackers and if there is a way to escape for you. **You then leave the area to a safer environment.**

Motivation to defend yourself must be **settled before the combat starts.** Don't go into a fight half-heartedly, **as this will get you killed.** If you decide to fight do so with **total commitment and ferocity. This might seem like a minor matter** but it's actually imperative because *any hesitation* in the street could get you killed so deciding beforehand whether you have the skill and commitment to deal with a life and death encounter is very important. Combining this with a righteous mindset and motivation is very important for victory.

Key Aspects of Combat

The stress of combat

The stress created by a combat situation is the response (autonomic reaction of the body and mind) that a combat situation elicits from you and your ability to control or minimize the body's response to this. This will *determine your success or failure to an extent*. To an extent because you can't stop a well-aimed bullet with just mindset – it involves a few factors and at some point, your decision-making process will be overcome by the intensity (call it confusion or fog of war) what I mean is your ability to change mentally and physically to the dynamic situation of combat. If you allow fear to overpower you could lose the confrontation due to its debilitating effects e.g., fear anger confusion, excitement or loss of focus are all part of the combat experience. Don't let these things control you, especially **fear** or **too much excitement** – stay focused on relaxation breathe deep. This can and should be *trained consistently to a point where it is a reflex.*

The amount that the fear affects you is determined by the amount of training you have done and your experiences when training. This doesn't mean you won't have an adrenaline dump as fear and adrenaline are not necessarily associated. You can get the adrenaline dump from the thought of potential action or the thought of you dealing with pain or danger. Therefore diminishing such thought patterns is a way to diminish the adrenaline effect.

Visualizing winning in your training sessions under *high pressure training* is how you condition your mind and body to relax when under stress. When training your body mental conditioning that you apply (mindset) in your mind as you are training is going to condition both your body to fight and your mind to win. This confidence that you build both mentally and physically translates into how you will fare and feel in a real-life situation to a degree because the adrenaline will affect you to some extent, which diminishes your ability some. Keep in mind a highly trained individual is less likely to be affected to the same extent by the negative effects of adrenaline (adrenal dump auditory exclusion and fixation) than an untrained person.

Some aspects of your preparation for combat work both ways such as ***deep breathing*** which allows you to relax. When your body is relaxed you can breathe normally and this allows your mind to work better and think better which allows you to win in a combat situation which will allow you to relax even more and therefore your breathing will be more relaxed relaxing your body even more. This is what brings you into a combat master zone of relaxation and focus (joy/exhilaration). This is why a professional fighter that has had 30 or 40 professional fights seems so much more relaxed than a new fighter, it is the ingrained reflex and experience of combat which allows the mind to relax and the body follows.

But don't be fooled – a professional fighter can be overcome by being too old and slow to use the experience he has learned so don't get too carried away or phased by an older experienced fighter. You still need your speed and agility to be good at combat. Where a more experienced fighter can win in a situation is through superior mindset and timing by timing, I mean he can foresee and react quicker than you because of experience. Good timing comes with experience and an ability to read the enemy. This might be less relevant in a situation where skills are the overarching element for victory e.g., in the case of speed and accuracy with a pistol or rifle, the deciding factor will be dexterity with the firearm which doesn't take a lot of fitness or power or athletic ability.

Any person who takes winning in a combat situation seriously **goes through scenarios in their mind** as to what they will do in an event of something happening. This helps the mind to think strategically, gives your mind something to work with in a combat environment. It makes you more familiar with strategic planning, and practice makes perfect. Strategic planning is another skill that your mind can learn to do better and faster with experience, as your mind is able to come to a conclusion about the veracity of your actions in any specific option quicker.

Mental and **physical** conditioning prevents this negative physical reaction to events that precipitates from the mind, which in turn causes the adrenal dump which can be out of fear. This response is due to the stress of combat (danger and potential pain) and to an extent conditioning of the mind over years through negative aspects of combat and crime (threats) can cause excessive stress associated with violence. This can be overcome and is achieved through visualization exercises. This is also overcome by doing physical drills continuous repetition of a movement while you apply the mindset and relaxation techniques that you were taught to keep your *body relaxed* and your *mind focused.*

The mental and physical association is what can either debilitate you or make you a winner. It is not so easy to just tell a person how the mental aspects affects the physical but they have to apply these aspects to know and understand how they work as well as apply them in combat. So the closest thing to combat will be training therefore it's up to the instructor to design course material and scenarios which bring the abilities out of the student.

One very debilitating aspect applied in some training courses is the stress test or stress inducer. If this is *done at the wrong time* during the training phase for the student's development then you will end up with a person that feels **stress just by the thought of a combat** scenario. This is clearly very bad for the student in real combat as it will diminish their ability to perform under combat conditions. The student needs to first be introduced to the concepts of dealing with combat stress then trained in these techniques then months later they can be stressed in a scenario. Doing this too early will just make the student too excited to perform optimally. If the person wants to perform in a very violent and dynamic situation they will need to be trained correctly when it comes to stress management.

Your **mind and body** are conditioned through the **gradual increase** in **stress stimuli**, such as a larger partner to train with more *realistic scenarios*, *intensity* in training such as *increase in speed of the movement* (maybe to failure depending on context). Intensity of the physical exercise (more reps and/or weight) in a gradual and ever-increasing way demanding more from your body and mind. **A gradual increase is the secret**; don't try to go too fast initially or you may injure yourself or lose *technical proficiency (technique)* and therefore **lose power,** *accuracy* and *efficiency*.

Remember *efficiency* is of the utmost importance in a combat situation as this produces power and, in the context of rifle shooting, speed of movement and accuracy to engage multiple targets. The efficiency is produced by using your core muscles to move and aim your weapon as they are large powerful muscles, which can move and stop your upper body the fastest. This is your shooting platform and your legs are your mobility. So keep this in mind – the core muscles aim and the legs move you; your eyes are for aiming and target acquisition.

Efficiency is the minimum amount of effort and strain for the maximum amount of effect, this applied in all forms of combat – unarmed, blade, pistol and rifle.

The stress from physical exertion and muscle fatigue which leads to **tiredness** is another aspect that can overcome your ability to concentrate and focus on the task at hand, and this is where efficiency normally breaks down due to fatigue. This is another area that needs to be addressed to be effective in fighting. This is when your fitness lets you down and you can't cope with the intensity or do the movement correctly any more. **Good technique** will allow you to still strike fairly hard, and shoot accurately even when you are tired.

You will notice mixed martial arts (MMA)/boxing fighters get diminished when they get tired, and can't execute a proper technique any more. One way to shoot more accurately when tired is to breathe in your lower abdomen; this stops your upper body from moving because when the chest heaves it disrupts your aim. Therefore breathing into the abdomen is best and needs to be trained to be useful in combat.

NB: Good technique is very important to functioning once you are out of energy and fighting for your life. This is why you should focus on your technique till it doesn't break down when under stress. You don't really have a choice either stay calm or die.

The Complete Warrior

What makes a complete warrior or a more prepared fighter? There are some factors:

General security considerations and societal indoctrinations

To have peace in your society you have to discern fact from fiction, and its pure fiction to think that taking away a person's ability to defend themselves will in any way help the crime situation. You would have to be totally corrupt or stupid to think this, yet people have been indoctrinated to believing this (disarming civilians such as in UK) is going to somehow make criminals less likely to attack and use a weapon against you. Time has borne this out – there are more knife attacks and even weapon (handgun) assaults in UK than in any time in history, this is directly as a result of the supposed weapons free society; the same happened in Australia.

No matter what type of excuse you use it just doesn't make logical sense to hand over the decision of whether you live or die to an already criminally minded (sometimes insane) person. The facts show us that it is literally the worst thing you can do, as you leave criminals with weapons, as happened in UK, Australia, Germany, France (terrorists killed unarmed French citizens and those citizens were totally defenseless and they were made so by their government) etc. In fact in Spain, Britain, Australia and France they had *terrorist attacks that could have been stopped by an armed citizen*. I would have a look at the agenda behind it and look at *the people* (the nation) behind it and make a decision on your plan of action. You will be surprised it will always be the same nation. As you will have noticed after disarming the population the whores of Satan basically started bring in millions of Muslims into the heart of Europe. Once you know the nation behind it you will know the source of all drug smuggling, child trafficking, porn and other demonic activity

Thousands of lives have been lost due to the negligence of governments by disarming their citizens. Thereby leaving their citizens *totally vulnerable to murder, rape and attack* of any type and any mischief, which a criminal wants to bring against the law-abiding citizen. That means *the responsibility of the government to protect its citizens by ensuring that they have the necessary capability to defend themselves* was <u>stolen</u> **from them in Germany, France, United Kingdom** and other European countries. This is a sign that your country is run by evil and not righteous men. Since these countries have applied this to their citizens their criminality overall has increased massively, but even if this were not the case it still doesn't give the government the right to disarm citizens.

Interesting historical fact: when the Romans said to the Germans give us your swords the Germans said **NO** *we won't be your slaves*. You wonder what the agenda behind the story is. If you take into consideration that after the European countries were disarmed, a certain group (nation) of people started pushing for bringing in third world savages and terrorists from Muslim countries.

Aspects of mental ability for effective combat

1. **Mindset**: Calm, Focused, Aggressive, Adapting
2. **Mental tools**: OAP (Observe, anticipate and plan)
3. **Mental rehearsal techniques**

Mindset is your attitude towards the combat situation and the opponent that in turn affects your physical performance whether negative or positive. For example it could or should be a cold calculated anger with a focused mind that is alert to the opponent's movement's actions and position. You could also call the mindset a **focused (focused mind) and relaxed aggression**. This is the opposite of a wild uncontrolled anger that can get you killed if you lose control over your facilities.

Watching the opponent, you fight accordingly this means a focused attention on their movements. You will notice some fighters have an uncanny ability to evade strikes even at a world class level; this is a **focused attention** able to detect subtle movements with a **relaxed body** (relaxed body of the fighter). Your mind cannot be busy with *any other thoughts* other than the enemy and your reaction to counter or nullify what they do and strike without thought (needs to be ingrained to unconscious level). This is only possible if you are relaxed and focused and react subconsciously – this must not be thought out but rather an instant reaction in order for it to work properly.

For example consider a street mugging (non-ambush scenario). To react properly to an attacker, you need to observe the attacker and not think "ok now I am going to do this or that" as that will open you up to surprise attacks. Instead, you either **attack first** or **wait with an intense and focused mind** but **relaxed body. Let your body move without the conscious thought process** – this will make you incredibly fast and unpredictable. This is only possible if you have done **thousands of repetitions** of the **proper** techniques beforehand such as a reverse punch or in boxing what might be called a right cross. The same applies to shooting situations where the focus on the attackers and subconscious shooting techniques apply.

The repetition and confidence come from being able to do a technique against an opponent that is ready and then it's easy against an enemy that is not ready for such a technique. If you decide to attack before he moves then it should be done with a relentless forward aggression. If in a situation where the only way out is to fight and winning is the only option.

Having explained how to observe the attacker in a combat situation, I would suggest attack is the best way to conclude a combat situation don't wait for him to attack you. If he is a good defensive fighter you might run in to a strike or blade or a bullet – judge for yourself at the time when to get into action. *There are no rules in combat* so you can do whatever you feel needs to be done to conclude the situation. There is no such thing as a dirty fighting technique – only effective and ineffective techniques.

The mindset of a well-practiced warrior is to <u>**not**</u> think too much of specific techniques but to **allow the mind to instinctively come to the correct conclusion** of what should be done to win in a combat situation. This is understood as '**no mind**' in Japanese fighting teaching but I would think that it is not a matter of having 'no thought process' but more to have **no specific technique in mind** – to react with what instinctively comes to mind. The more you train the correct technique and tactics the better your instinctive reaction will be. **The more you train** and the **better your quality of training** the **better will be your decision-making process.**

No system that teaches a particular technique for such and such an attack and a different technique for another attack, is going to be effective. By this I mean when you have 100 different attack angles and a 100 different defense options in some systems. Your mind will be unable to search through all these – instead you need a simple solution for most attacks. Your mind might not be able to access the specific technique you were taught in class if there is a plethora of options, so **keep it simple**.

To put this in perspective, it will look like this: if an assailant wants to stab you, punch him in the face with correct technique and you have a great chance of winning; if he has a grenade punch him in the face if he has a pistol punch him in the face after redirecting the barrel and so on. Simple and proven effective this is direct and easy to learn. I have used it so many times I have lost count. It works and there are no doubts if you know how to punch you can be 90% effective. You can't be 100% sure because you never know who you are fighting such as a maybe a boxer who can take a punch.

Combat is too flexible (varied) for that type of rigid mindset. You must have done thousands of repetitions of movement, drawing of your weapon, striking and manipulation. I find it much more useful to teach an understanding of combat and then do simple techniques that can be applied in multiple scenarios. For example do thousands of repetitions of techniques known to actually work in realistic combat scenarios then teach the mindset of being calm but aggressive?

You should be moving in a dynamic way that is smooth and balanced with no specific thoughts, thereby allowing your mind to reach an instinctive reaction (conclusion) to an attack. Your primary goal is to switch off the control of the attacker's body which is via his brain. This is better done with superior accuracy with reasonable speed and intensity.

This is not always possible as you sometimes barely have time to ID (identify) the attacker. You will be presenting a weapon and shooting in maybe 1.5-2 sec (highly trained shooters can draw and shoot in under a 1 sec but the shock factor can sometimes mitigate this speed). That means you are grateful to get center mass shots on target as time will sometimes only allow for this and some of the time you will be grateful to even get a hit on target at all if the attack is totally unexpected. This is because your brain is first trying to identify whether it's a problem or not and then it's trying to identify the attacker. These factors make it difficult to act immediately and this causes a delay in reaction by you to the attack. This is one of the reasons attacks are as successful as the attackers have such an advantage over anyone untrained and unsuspecting.

Righteous thought patterns promote survival

Understanding why you fight or defend your family and friends is very important in righteous action. This is because any hesitation can get you killed and *seconds count* so *determine this beforehand.*

If you are wondering about whether you should be carrying a blade/or the modern day equivalent the pistol then go read Luke Chapter 22 verse 36 in the Christian Bible. One of the reasons or a contributing factor is the inculcated mindset of having no weapon is somehow beneficial to survival; this has been introduced by the communists in the school system and universities. This is a contributing factor but not the only reason we have such a massive crime rate in South Africa. the mindset indoctrinated and inculcated by the universities and learning institutions backed and sponsored by people and organization with a lack of respect of GOD and our GOD given right to self-defense. This brings about the misunderstanding that if you are not armed then criminals will be nice to you. This is **fantasy of the highest order** because you are more likely to lose your life if you have no way of defending yourself. This type of fantasy is called **wanton stupidity** or being stupid to **facilitate your own agenda.** This is happening so many times all around where these people are working on making people really dumb to reality. Thousands of people die in these countries because their governments are taken over by shadow groups behind the scenes.

Basically, the criminals can't believe what a fool you are to be unarmed it's so much easier for them to steal from an unarmed citizen that an armed citizen. Think about it – if you were a criminal, **would you want to attack an armed person** or an unarmed one? The real criminal's in this type of scenario are the governments that help the criminal's by helping them indirectly by disarming the law abiding

The South African government seems to be more occupied with the law-abiding citizen as it has not occurred to them that it is the criminals that are involved with crime. It's what is called "when your **gardener** becomes **your president**" a distinctly African problem.

It's a difficult one to work out especially for the head of the police; he thinks having law abiding citizens unarmed might help? And of course, the police don't mind arming the criminals or gangs basically the criminals are an extension of the government (as our governing party was once listed as a terrorist organization).

To **not** be a target in combat/SHTF type scenario, you need at least 3 of the following (if you have all 6 of these points trained in or part of your character then you are a hard target):

1. A weapon, not obvious or openly as this can attract trained or desperate individuals
2. Training, in intensity, speed and accuracy under duress
3. Correct mindset
4. Awareness
5. Decisive, aggressive and rapid reactions
6. Assess your environment and your performance and at a later date correct any shortcomings.

The psychology of winning and science of victory

Correct training principles bring about a positive mindset by experience and conditioning of the mind and body as a unit. This is through experience of techniques working in training and therefore the winning mindset is reinforced. Furthermore using your techniques in varied situations further reinforces this correct mindset. This is due to the decision-making process that you need to work through when you are presented with multiple options to choose from and can make good decisions leading to a reasonable outcome.

The techniques need to be **trained to instinct** (repetition of the correct technique). ***Techniques that are understood and can be applied without conscious thought***, and are applicable to real life situations will be useful for self-protection, taking into consideration how people attack, in particular the intensity and forward momentum of the attack. As well as understanding how people react when being shot. It's not always as you think it might be as some people barely show a response at all and some drop like a stone. It's got to do with shot placement and the psychology of the individual that dictates how they react to the impact.

To **train something to an instinctive level**, it is recommended you do at least **4000 repetitions** to be able to apply a specific technique in a real situation. Keep in mind, also ingrain the mindset that goes with combat. The number of repetitions to acquire high levels of skill is only a generalization – it could be far less for a person with natural inclination for martial prowess but on average it's going to take a lot of repetition. I have seen where some people take a year to reach a fairly high standard and then can go on to train themselves and they get really good with the foundational understanding inculcated of what constitutes a good tactic technique and procedure to prevail in combat.

Mindset and how the brain affects your actions

The mind can either assist or detract from your ability to function in a fight. That is why we focus a lot on the mental attitude of the student and constantly reinforce the "mindset" attitude.

A misunderstood concept is that you have muscle memory; this is incorrect because your muscle cannot remember but what does happen is the information stored in the cerebellum (repetition allows neural pathways to be ingrained) is more easily accessible to you in a fight if you have done enough repetitions for this information to become more of a subconscious function than a thought-out action. So a more appropriate term for this function is to say how to develop subconscious memory function or stress memory function and this is found in the cerebral cortex which is closer to the nerves of the body than the actual brain.

This area is closest to your spinal column which allows your body to access the information quicker than an untrained person. It will also have something to do with the brain's understanding of the movements of an attacker how it looks (how the brain interprets the movement) for a person to attack and the *subtle signs* a person's body will give off before an attack. These subconscious memory patterns and techniques will also speed up your reaction to an attack.

This is because you are reacting to subtle signs that another person might not pick up this is the same for sparring with a person that has very little training and you might be a 'black belt' that allows you to see what others can't see. An experienced fighter knows a lot about the subject of combat and can see the subtle signs. For example, in a "street" situation this might be as subtle as picking up an opponent's front foot moving first. This is because you can see their whole body due to relaxation and a 'soft' (wide view) visual focus technique. This small and subtle sign helps you to move first or simultaneously. If too much tension is present your pupil will constrict and the field of view will change and narrow everything down hurting your chances.

The reality of how your mind reacts to stress is dictated by the **amount** of training time period of training, intensity of training and the *quality* and number of repetitions you have done during training. The quality of your training will lead to fast accuracy and this is what brings about the confidence. What is quality training, now that is debatable but let's say it must be realistic in application and fit into the time constraints of real combat.

Quality also refers to the training received with regards to **reality-based tactics, techniques and procedures** as opposed to training based on a figment of someone's imagination. Never underestimate the importance of the flexible mindset training. You will also realize as you gain experience with teaching is that *good technique* seems to stay with the student and there is *little loss in accuracy* even *after a long time of abstinence* from training.

This is only applicable if you have adequate training to override all other natural responses that might have been in your subconscious. Bad or inadequate technique tends to leave you with bad accuracy after a hiatus in your training such as a year or 2 of abstinence. It does take time to develop these skills to the level where they are subconscious but once you reach this level then you will more likely hold onto them for a long time. What will happen though is you will lose speed and accuracy as these tend to degrade with time if you don't practice them consistently.

Has the instructor taken into consideration the time-distance relationship e.g., can the technique you are doing have the ability to fit into the time it takes for the attacker to attack you? An illustration of this would be making 2 or 3 moves in the time the attacker does one downward strike with a blade. **Logic** says this would be impractical (even impossible) in real life fighting situations, this is because there is a maximum speed with which you can move your limbs. This means if he is moving at maximum speed and you are moving at maximum speed. This is within reason a boundary for speed and can only overcome with extensive training for speed and superior mindset. This will even have its limits due to the reduced ability that is induced by adrenaline (tension/fear).

Does it fit into *full speed training* and can the technique still be applied? That's why what is done in combat varies to what is taught in the classroom or training range. The further away from real war the military of a country is the more fanciful the training becomes due to human nature and the danger and nature of real combat training are lost in time. It could also be due to influx of persons involved with the training that do not have the necessary combat experience which leads to fanciful training strategies.

Highly trained warriors do not experience the fight or flight symptoms *to the same extent* as an untrained person would. It might be that some of the symptoms will affect the trained warrior but **not to the same extent** and sometimes very little if at all depending on the extent of the confrontation and the training that was done by the defender (operator). This can also be affected by the length of time since training seriously for combat if it's still fresh in your mind and your body is in good condition then you should deal well with an attack with greater ease than if you were unfit.

If you don't have time to think about an attack and it happens out of the blue then you tend to react well if your training for combat is comprehensive and intense enough that your mind works in the attack level of intensity. This is probably because the mind and body function subconsciously to come to a defense strategy and there is no time to clutter the mind with irrelevant thoughts.

The instructor should at certain intervals reinforce mindset and incorporate exercises to make the student more aware of their mindset and help to reinforce the process of consciously relaxing breathing deeply, staying confident thinking of what they must do and **not the attacker can do to harm them**. It will behave (appropriate) you to have this mindset and to do the same on your course during training or even when you train on your own reinforcing and using your mindset with tactics or procedures that will help you in a fight. This doesn't mean you don't watch the enemy with focus and relaxed attention as what they do will determine your reaction to an extent. It's just that your mind cannot be focused on unnecessary thoughts if you want to survive a contact.

Training Principles for Teaching Combat

Keep in mind when reading this manual that for the sake of brevity we cannot cover all areas or aspects of weapon use and every type and technique with regards to weapon retention or disarming, as the manual would just be too long. I have tried to keep it simple and with only the essentials for combat and survival in single operator situations. If you have very little time available to train then *train the basics* as these will keep you alive in most situations. You really only need to be fast and accurate and this will stand you in good stead for most combat situations. I have specified the basics for good combat ability below, as they are the most critical for combat efficiency.

The principles of effective training

Knowing and understanding the ***basics of the specific discipline*** you want to learn is what makes you good at that discipline.

It is said that **to be a master** in a specific discipline you need to do at least **10 000 hours** of training. This is not as simple in self-defense because the person will have to spend 10 000 hours **of the correct techniques tactics** and **mindset** to be a master at combat as these are essential to success. Personally, I think that it is a bit of an exaggeration as I have seen people get very proficient in pistol and rifle with 3-4 hours training on weekends over a period of about 1-2 years. It also won't help you to have 10 000 hours of kung-Fu because we have seen supposed masters getting beaten by an MMA fighter with much less hours of training than the master. There is a reason for this and it is that some systems are not geared for combat. A more accurate amount of time to become proficient with a weapon for self-defense is probably closer to 300-600 hours of training and 3-6 years. What can speed up the process is correct and realistic training techniques that actually work with a good understanding being imparted to the student.

As with all things in life the number of hours the person will have to practice will depend largely on the person who's being taught it could be a lot less than 10 000 hours, it might be as low as ***500 hours*** for some. Note that you might not be a master of combat but you can have ***excellent skills***. From my experience, a person can have exceptional expertise and skill with 4-8 hors training a week over a period of 3-6 years depending on the person's age, athleticism, time available to train, motivation, focus and intelligence.

Realize that a person can have useful wisdom and yet lack technical proficiency and understanding of certain aspects of mechanically operated devices. We can think of such people as having positive "street smarts" but perhaps lacking certain academic skills.

Do not allow **negative thoughts** to dominate your thinking as *they will affect your performance* <u>negatively</u> through subtle tension building up in your body. Instead, focus on strategy and moving to your advantage. Even better than thinking of strategy is to have a predetermined combat strategy that is simple and effective. Negative thoughts are usually as a result of previous experience (bad situations) and lack of preparation. Negative thoughts will tense you up and cause you to slow down; this can be debilitating and should be avoided at all costs.

Expect to win and use positive reinforcement continually. This is done until it becomes second nature. Do this in training so that you more than likely do it in a real-life situation.

Stay mentally focused but **physically relaxed**. This means the mind is focused and adapting to what the enemy is doing and the body is relaxed to move fast and think better. Watch people and the situation around you carefully using the acronym OAP (as explained earlier). Awareness gives you a few seconds longer to react if you notice any attackers and allows you to mentally prepare or brace even if it's only a second or two.

Remember <u>every</u> **(not some) opponent has a weakness** and is to some degree apprehensive of you whether they show it or not. It's the person that ignores and overrides these feelings and replaces them with either excitement or positive thoughts that stands the most chance of winning. Laughing is a good way to relax and fight better try it next time and you will be amazed. The attacker might think you are insane and become unsettled; it's unnerving to see someone that could die any second smiling or laughing at this point in time, think carefully about that. Any time an attacker is scared gives you the advantage, let that sink in ☺ .

Perhaps use a key word or a phrase to get your mind into a focused mode e.g., if you're facing muggers or any enemy think something like "breathe deep" or whatever your "go to" word is, you might even exclaim it outwardly. This is not essential because you can just breathe deeply and consciously relax your body to get focused. Focus is a state of being **physically relaxed** and mentally **aware of your surroundings (environment) and attacker.**

Reduce the stress you experience by applying visualization exercises during your training i.e., before any combat situation arises. This is because in your visualization you will overcome and win and this will set you up with a better mindset. Correctly applied visualization will have a lot of detail in it to bring about the desired result. It should be done daily for a couple of months to prepare your mind for combat. Training with a combat mindset with the correct focus on physical and mental aspects prepares you for combat.

Use fewer techniques and *become proficient in these techniques* to bring your reaction time down. The reason your reaction time will be faster is because your mind will have a basic response to most attacks and this will help you be less confused as to a plan of action. Confusion is your enemy, so *simplicity of tactic and technique* is therefore your friend, as is instant reaction to an attack. To win with your firearm, you need a good "center mass" hit that causes incapacitation quickly which is not the same for every person except in cases where a brain stem shot is executed. A quick and accurate draw or presentation of the rifle with a well-placed incapacitating shot is what it takes.

For example: awareness means you can ID the attacker (that's the OAP = observe anticipate plan, which is a mental tool) you then move laterally, draw your firearm simultaneously ID the target as the person might either not be an attacker or even an innocent (or who may not be the attacker you saw earlier in a prolonged situation), engage if the person turns out to be the enemy, then check your environment. This will increase your confidence when you are able to quickly and efficiently do target identification.

Here is another example of what I mean in a context of a street fight, of course it takes a good bit of time to perfect your striking technique but once you have it you will and can keep it for life your defense strategy looks like this: strike to the ***groin knee to the head*** then finish with a more deadly (incapacitating) strike such as a throat strike or eye jab or rear of the ***neck strike***. The neck especially the rear of the neck is filled with nerves and the spine is filled with smaller and more delicate bones than the rest of the spine and is very vulnerable to a strike with the ulna bone of the forearm which is a fairly strong bone and is capable of causing pain and incapacitating a person.

This is especially important when faced with a close opponent where you can't draw your pistol immediately as this might allow the attacker to grab your weapon. I remember a particularly successful strike to the back of the neck when grabbed by someone in an alley when 5 men failed in their attempt to mug me. That one strike gave me the ascendancy, instantly incapacitating my nearest attacker, and they quickly realized it was futile to continue their attack once I could draw my knife to counter their knives.

Keeping your techniques to a minimum also allows you to train those aspects of your combat strategy more than if you try to learn 50 ways to disarm a blade or gun. This doesn't mean just one technique but more an understanding of ***how and why a technique works*** and then allowing a certain amount of flexibility as each person is different and getting them to adapt is of great importance. Anecdotal evidence is the fact that in the 70 street situations 60-70 % of the time a simple fast and accurate punch can finish the fight. Now keep in mind they were not raving lunatics high on some drug.

Keeping the number of techniques to a minimum

1. This will give you more time for the *basics.*
2. You can do more repetitions of those techniques you know work.
3. Less fatigue due to hours needed to get good at basic technique.
4. Less chance of injury as it's easier to learn and apply one basic technique, the more you do the technique the better.
5. You will have a more in-depth understanding of the techniques you know with more intimacy. This will lead to more accuracy over the long run, don't change your technique every few months as you set yourself back more than you realize.
6. Doing the *basics perfectly* is what makes you good which leads to mastery and deadly accuracy.
7. More time for those essential techniques that are proven to be effective, the secret is getting training from someone who knows the difference between techniques that work and these that don't.

Attitudes and expectations can play a role in your performance so a positive attitude will mostly bring about a positive outcome as far as this is humanly possible and your training has allowed for the performance that will be needed. Performance is dictated by speed, agility, accuracy, mobility combined with strategy and mindset.

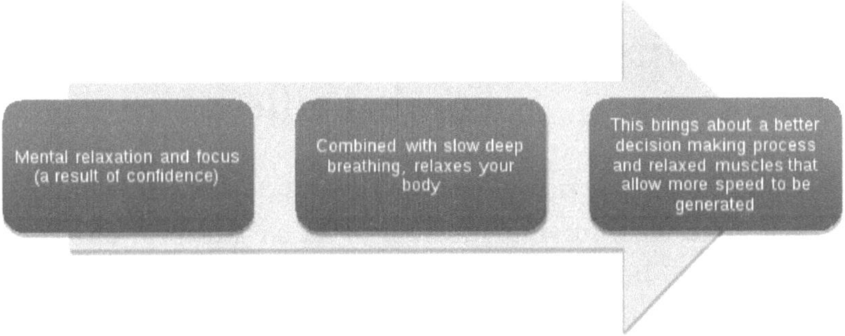

Mental relaxation and focus (a result of confidence)
Combined with slow deep breathing, relaxes your body
This brings about a better decision making process and relaxed muscles that allow more speed to be generated

Objective of training principles for combat rifle

This is to prepare the student for physical confrontation in the street/war zone, in a survival situation or in an attack in any theatre of operations. The techniques and tactics are not all expedient for teams but in some cases can be used for team members; if all the members of the team train together and *understand the dynamic nature of the techniques then it is possible to use them for combat teams.*

Is it better to know yourself or to know your enemy, which is more important?

Both are equally important: know yourself, weaknesses and strong points, change habits that are bad for your combat ability. And know your enemy's weak points and tactics and techniques, as in this way you can plan how to defeat them before you even make contact.

General overview of training principles

169

Moving targets

If possible have moving targets made available to the operators, as everything will be dynamic in reality. In reality the person does not wait for you to shoot them they will try to take cover so only shooting stationary targets is not good enough.

Use your imagination have moving targets behind cover and some in the open.

Practice being in the moment when the skill training is finished and you do scenario training, by this I mean let yourself relax and let your self-act instinctively.

Fallacies about combat training

Here is a list of common fallacies regarding training for combat:

1. You can do a 3-day weapons course and you will be effective. In reality, it takes years to get really good and there is no shortcut to excellence.

    a. To get a reasonable understanding of **unarmed combat**, **blade**, **pistol** or **rifle** should take the average student about 2 to 4 hours per week per subject for 3 years. So, if each subject is given 4 hours per week and there are 4 subjects then you could say it will take at least 2 hour x 52 weeks x 3 years x 4 subjects = 1248 hours of training to be fairly well versed in the 4 major subjects for self-defense. These are guidelines as different people learn at different rates and they have different background knowledge and physical capabilities, which either assists or detracts from the speed of learning. It is easier to learn pistol and rifle than it is to learn unarmed combat because of the fitness, speed, power, flexibility and strength required in unarmed combat.

    b. What really helps to speed up the process is to have a good understanding of what makes a person accurate (grip, stance, weapon presentation) mobile, dynamic and with correct mindset. The key is *concentrating on the basics* and drilling them to instinct and then only developing the more complex or advanced aspects when the person has the basics mastered.

    c. ***A master is the person who has mastered the basics.***

1. **You can use any shooting stance and grip, with any arm position and they will all work equally well in combat.** Having said that the combat stance with one foot forward and the one foot backwards will be a little more stable and will allow more control for recoil. Even though some stances will work to an extent you should find the technique which allows you to use the least energy (most efficient). This causes the least fatigue and allow you to point with the rifle instinctively finding your sights quickly for close and long ranges. *Any technique that causes stress or tension is probably wrong and will fatigue you out in the long run and is bad for real combat, as you should have as little tension induced by your technique as possible.* Here are realistic issues regarding stance and grip:

   a. We know from real life that a stance where the rifle stock is in the position of pressing on the shoulder does not perform as well positioning the stock on the pectoral muscles close to the sternum (center bone of chest) for 'instinctive' shooting. The latter allows better recoil management. This is due to the amount of weight behind the stock to control recoil – if someone pushes on your shoulder it's easier to move it off line, but if the person pushes on your center of mass then it is more difficult for them to destabilize you. It's a basic fact of physics that any force applied to the center of mass (center of gravity) does not alter the attitude (angle, position) of the object it might merely move the object along the line of force. Whereas forces applied off-center do change the attitude and in fact the further the force is away from the center the more easily the object can be repositioned. In this case the rifle recoil is the force and shouldering the rifle too far from your center. This makes your fire very much less accurate, especially when using rapid shot sequences.

b. The centerline stock position increases your chances of survival because it has less to go wrong.

c. It's even better if your stock is **short enough** so you can put the stock in the middle of the pectoral muscles, as this then puts the rifle sight in line with your aiming eye and allows a more natural sight alignment with less stress on the neck muscles. This will allow you to go for a longer period without fatigue. This is another reason that "bull pup" style rifles are easier to manipulate than an assault rifle of standard design.

d. The rifle can also be brought higher so the stock is fairly high on the pectoral muscles, which means you don't have to lower your head too much and put stress on the neck muscles. Staining too much will cause tension and the tension will cause fatigue.

2. **If you train hard enough you can fight effectively against a person with a gun or blade while you are unarmed**. While this is possible, your chances of survival are minimal. Avoid unarmed combat because the percentage chances of success are 10-20% or less depending on your skill level (strategy and tactics), your age, strength, speed and reflexes. To reach a level to take on a person skilled with a knife takes years. You will need speed, power, agility, and correct techniques for unarmed gun or knife defense. In reality you will need to strike the attacker to "switch them off". And most people lack understanding of high quality striking techniques.

a. **Reality: It is always best to use a gun against an armed attacker.** You are much less likely to sustain any damage if you react to the attack quickly enough; your reaction was initiated when the person was far enough.

b. Use a blade if you don't have a gun. Only in a last-ditch effort use your hands against an armed attacker.

c. You increase your survivability when you use a weapon against an attacker instead of your hands. If you use your hands you will need to attack as much as possible with maximum aggression and striking areas that cause maximum damage (throat, groin, neck, joints, eyes etc.).

3. **You can train <u>low intensity</u> in your training environment and apply your tactics in a high intensity high threat environment**. This would be the equivalent of training by doing marathons in order to be good at sprints. This would clearly put you at a disadvantage as intensity affects the speed of movement which is more power orientated (more muscular contraction) as you move faster and the mind has to think/act faster which is a skill in itself. The way speed affects movement is that as muscles tense up it changes the arc and size of the moving parts of your body; it is easier to do a small movement fast than a large movement fast. The mind plays a huge role in speed of the movement and your ability to move fast.

a. **Reality:** You will likely die if you don't do high intensity training. Yes, for beginners you start off slowly to get the basics and mechanics correct. Then gradually increase the intensity of movements and scenarios. This applies both long term and short term. "Short term" means build up the intensity over a period of 30 minutes to 1 hour and "long term" is pushing a little harder over the period of 1 year.

    b. You need to do it to increase your combat speed (especially your maximum pace) and this will also help your hand eye coordination at speed. Your mind gets used to the speed and the coordination becomes easier.

4. **You can learn 5 to 10 techniques in one day and then go out and remember them and apply them in a real situation**. This is the kind of training you might do on a short course of 2-3 days. If you do a short course, it's more advantageous to do *fewer techniques* and *learn them well* than to do many and not know any of them well. For instance, learning a particular weapon disarm for a whole day and make sure you fully understand as many aspects as possible before going on to the next technique. You can't be a pro athlete in a 3 days, 3 weeks or 3 months, so you can't be a deadly combatant either.

    a. **Reality:** It's only possible to learn well if the student goes off and trains the techniques on their own for a period of 6 months to 1 year or more. This is to make any technique a subconscious action without thought or deliberation.

    b. But even then, they will need *guidance* (technique correction) because doing repetitions of the wrong technique could be more damaging to their long-term training goals.

5. **You can do some half-hearted little punch in a close encounter as weapon retention and that will work in combat**. In reality, this type of striking will likely get you killed. *I see this a lot*, either due to misunderstanding of striking technique or misunderstanding of how hard you need to strike in close quarters to be victorious.

a. **Reality:** To be effective you need to traumatize the attacker to the extent that they have a change of mind or they are **incapacitated** for a long enough period of time to allow you to do something else, that might include a throat strike, groin kick or strike the back of the neck etc.

6. **Smooth is fast.** This might be good if you have a stack of 20 soldiers standing behind you to cover you, but this is not applicable in most combat situations. This is why we train speed (intensity specifically to reinforce neuromuscular (nerves in the muscles) pathways). Power movements speed up the mental aspects of hand eye coordination. Slow and deliberate training is only done in the initial phase of all training to make sure the students perform the technique properly. This could be 6 months to 1 year, then once the techniques are ingrained it's time for speed and intensity. As mentioned before, it's necessary to increase the intensity slowly.

   a. **Reality:** In combat, **fast is alive and slow is dead** (this must be balanced with control and accuracy and these two are controlled by realization and calm i.e., mindset). This doesn't mean you have to go so fast you lose control, but speed is very important and should be trained as an aspect of combat preparation. This is especially important if you are training for combat as an individual combatant.

<u>Important note:</u> Training for combat must always consist of all aspects of combat functions (purposes). Concepts such as physical exertion, mental aspect, tactics and intensity and where possible a bit of chaos or "fog of war" (chaos with control) if that is possible. These allow the student to improve all areas that affect their performance in

a combat environment. You could see this as the prerequisites for all combat training including weapons type training such as rifle, pistol – even knife and unarmed training will use and perform with these aspects of combat. The lack of fitness strength and *stamina* will always count against you in a combat situation if you lack any of these; this is why *keeping a basic standard of fitness is important.* For example, a 5km run 4-5 times per week with 2-3 sessions of full body calisthenics per week is a decent baseline. Of fitness.

Criteria for effective combat performance

These are some areas of physical performance criteria that need to be addressed to be effective in combat but this list is not exhaustive:

1. *Speed:* movement of the limbs and the forward or sideways movement of the whole body. The speed that you can move your limbs at is directly related to your strength and physical conditioning. You will never be able to move the upper body with maximum speed and efficiency if you don't have very good core strength. Specifically your core muscles and or muscles of the torso which would be but not limited to: external and internal oblique's, transverse abdominis, rectus abdominis and the back muscles which support but not necessarily part of the initial of movement e.g., spinae erector muscles and quadratus lumbered.

2. *Intensity:* of the mind and body movement as a unit. This is both a mental and physical exercise as movement and speed with which your mind can function is related to the amount of intensity training you have done as the more intensity you do the faster your mind and body get as a coordinated unit due to the conditioning of the muscles ligaments and tendons. This is also related to and associated with the brain's ability to skip over the thinking process of the movement as it will become second nature once it is done enough times. This then allows the brain to focus on other aspects such as target acquisition and where to move as the body automatically accesses the weapon without a conscious thought process.

3. *Muscle endurance: the ability to lift a fairly light weight multiple times e.g.,* raising your rifle up to your shoulder 20 to 30 times will take muscles endurance. This is conditioned by doing high repetition weights or manual labor with fairly

light weights e.g., say your "1 repetition max" is 20 kg for your deltoid (shoulder muscle) then doing 3-5 sets of 20-30 reps with 5 kg will not build size but rather strength and endurance. Muscle endurance is more important for speed than heavy weights, as with heavy weights you build strength with too much mass, and mass can slow you down (harder for your body to move with the extra weight). Therefore you want increased strength without too much mass to be efficient and stronger, pound for pound of muscles weight.

4. ***Cardio fitness:*** the ability to run for at least 30 minutes to 1 hour or more and to be able to function after the event. ***Minimum*** cardio you can do to still be fairly fit is 20 mins 3 times a week. Call this a baseline (minimum core fitness). To be reasonably cardio fit you could get away with doing 4 days of 30 mins of running at a low intensity pace. To be combat fit you need to run at least 5 days a week 30 - 45 mins at a time. Keep in mind rest is just as important as training hard because with no rest you will only break down. To take it to the next level you will need to add some speed training into the whole conditioning program. Speed increases your fitness quicker but can also bring on overtraining faster.

   a. The program will look something like this: Mon/Wed/Fri you can run in evenings 5 km (fairly hard run); Tuesday and Thursday morning do light 5 km run with 5-10 sprints in the evening.

   b. Muscular conditioning will look something like this: using 30-40 % of your maximum weight you do on Mon/Wed/Fri either after the run or in the morning, whole body conditioning. The sets can be anything from 2-5 sets (I would keep it to 2-3 sets), because you will do every major muscle group e.g., push up (bench press) uses all large pushing muscles:

pecs, triceps and anterior deltoid. A pulling exercise such as chins (latissimus pull down) will focus on most large muscles such as bicep, latissimus, posterior deltoid (rhomboids and trapezius will be stabilizers). Pushing with the legs such as squats, done with the feet at different widths and feet at different angles, will work all large leg muscles such as rectus femoris, vastus lateralis, or intermedius and medialis. The number of reps will depend on the person's strength and conditioning and could vary from 10-20 repetitions and as high as 30 to 40 for well-conditioned athletes. Once again, don't go according to what others are doing – your genetic makeup is different and this is why you should go according to your own needs.

5. ***Timing:*** *this can apply to efficiency when changing a rifle magazine or watching the attacker and knowing when to counter* (both a physical and mental process as the body has to keep up with the mind). Timing is normally improved by repetitions as well as physical speed and power exercises. Let it happen – any thought process involved will slow you down, so just let it happen with a clear mind.

6. ***Balance:*** your ability to maintain equilibrium while moving, to maintain balance. This is normally a ***function of the core muscles*** and general muscle strength. Flexibility does help, and the ability to relax helps as the antagonistic muscles are more at rest than if they were tensed (as when doing a contraction). Use only the prime movers such as the quadriceps and minimize the effect of the counter balancing muscles which would be the hamstring (also called the antagonistic muscles). Like any skill you want to develop doing more training in that discipline will help here so do

exercises to improve your balance.

7. ***Core strength:*** in your stabilizing muscles which also effects your balance will also affect your ability to punch with power and how long you can carry a backpack, your running ability by stabilizing your hips during running. Deadlift capacity and many other functions. Core strength is actually the core of all abilities when it comes to strength, agility and power (sprinting). Doing exercise such as hyperextensions and sit-ups help but are not specific core strength exercises. Deadlifts and planks will build the core more specifically.

8. ***Specific muscle development:*** weapon retention grip strength would be forearm muscles. These can be strengthened by doing weapon handling or punching exercise for striking focus on transverse abdominis, and oblique's. Quadriceps and glutei muscles help for walking long distances. Sprinting uses mostly the gluteus and hamstrings as they are the "pull through" muscles. Spinae erector muscles are for backpacking, as well as rectus abdominis (stomach muscles).

9. ***Flexibility***: the ability of your limbs to do a large range of movement without stress and tension, that is within the body's natural range of maximum motion. The joints have a limit and should not be over stepped if you want good health, the legs have a ball and socket joint and any excessive range of motion can damage the edge of the joint. Flexibility allows ***fluid movement*** *and* ***prevents injury***. It also allows you to move fast in a more relaxed state and therefore helps with speed and execution of full techniques.

10. ***Repetition:*** of the correct technique, tactics and procedures with combat mindset done multiple times to the extent where the mind does not play a role in conscious thought of what to do in the action. Repetition allows the mind to work on any little flaws in a given technique and strengthens the

associated muscles. As time goes on and you do more repetitions your mind concentrates on your surroundings as your hands and muscles start to react subconsciously.

The above are the physical aspects. You have to cater for the mental training as well, such as mental preparation in mindset and mental tools which deal with how your mind observes and processed the information in your environment. This includes the way you deal with the stress of combat, and is why it is imperative to include scenarios where stress is induced and the person is forced to overcome it:

Mindset acronym to apply for combat

How point aim works

1. When you draw, punch the weapon to be in **line with your eyes** so that you are looking at the target with the weapon superimposed over the target.
2. You must line up the whole weapon – do not use the sights on the target. There is a difference between sighting and pointing, when you use the sights you try to see them and this takes your attention of the area as a whole in front of you. When you line them up you look at the target and do not use the sights even though they are lined up with your eye and target in a straight line. This means you need to use sighted aim for long shots only, and then you can use the sights by focusing on them as the alignment stays the same.
3. Concentrate on the trigger as this will make the difference whether you shoot accurately or not. Mistakes that occur a lot from an incorrect trigger pull are shooting down which could be anticipation or pushing the weapon left because of the finger that is placed on the trigger is pushing from right to left.
4. Watch the target or targets and see what happens as this will give you a tactical appreciation of the developing situation. This is for many reasons one of which is the person (attacker) could still be a viable attacker, this is also because other enemy could also be around, weapons might be within reach of the attacker that you just engaged etc.

Picture sequence for <u>anticipation</u> when shooting the pistol follows.

A dummy round is mixed with live rounds so when the dummy chambers, any muzzle drop caused by the student flinching will be evident. The drop will translate to about 6 inches at 10 meters even though it's only a few mm at the gun. The drop is indicated with a red line annotated on the images.

Figure 1

Picture showing draw path (red) relative to sighting plane (blue):

The draw path should a direct line to the sighting plane for quickest times – no excessive lifting or looping movements should occur.

Point aim is for close engagements

1. One of the most neglected points is that in almost 70% (maybe as high as 90% in self-defense shooting) of your fights, your range from the attacker will be about **1- 5 meters**. That means 70% of your training should be close range between 1-10 meters and most of it only out to 5 meters with a lot of speed and fast target acquisition.

1. In fact, sometimes the attacker will be so close you will need to draw and **shoot from the hip**. This is a very specific skill and needs to be trained so that your brain understands where the barrel is pointing when you can't see the weapon, this should not be so difficult because the attacker is very close like 1-2 meters if you are shooting from the hip

1. Affective point aim only works if you use the correct **shooting structure**. That means the whole body position must be correct. This is of course very difficult in reality because the attacker normally dictates the time when you need to draw as you will be reacting to the attacker, but this is not always the case because, your awareness might have dictated that you can engage before the attacker sees you

1. You are more likely to use point aim in any event in a close range gunfight as the adrenaline won't allow you to look at the sights as the attacker is what you will look at. This is due to both physiological and psychological effects of the adrenaline rush during an attack. This is for an surprise attack because if it was seen beforehand then you would have time to plan and prepare, which means you might act more controlled and be able to use your sights

1. **The objective of point aiming** is to allow you to **quickly engage two or more assailants** while focusing on your targets and what they are doing in front of you and not on your front sight. This might not be initially apparent as you spend most (99%) of your time shooting non-reactive targets that don't shoot back or move to their advantage. This means you don't realize how important it is to watch and shoot to make split second adjustments to your target's acquisition and tracking

1. This is only meant for very close range shooting, 5 to 10 meters, and if you are practicing regularly then up to 15 meters for a body shot. To get hits further than this you have to have a very good structure. What I call **shooting with your structure**. Keep in mind the whole shooting structure must stay the same both in combat training and in a fight so that you can rely on the results of that structure. If you find that you can't hit targets out to 8-10 meters with point aim then your shooting structure is not correct and not consistent.

1. Another reason point aim is essential is because during the fight or flight response the contour of the eyes' lenses change in an attempt to take in more information, the pupils dilate resulting in the loss of ability to focus on close range objects such as your gun sights. This will be especially relevant in a close range encounter. If the range is further out and you don't have the same adrenaline rush then you might be able to use your sights. This is possible with correct type of training and extensive correct training with intensity.

1. Your mind whether you want to or not will be wholly focused on pointing and pulling the trigger because your brain is

stressed and you want to engage the enemy as fast as possible, this will be subconscious. That is why most times a person will shoot a number of rounds if faced with a fast and aggressive attack. If you have time to anticipate the attack then you might have a more controlled counter attack with only shooting a few rounds such as 2 -3 rounds being delivered by you.

1. You might have heard this before: train like you would fight. That means train with intensity, focus, techniques and tactics but remember your mindset for training for the street. This does not only means the intensity aspects of combat but also the physical aspects such as how your body reacts to stress for example you will lower your center of gravity without conscious thought to make yourself a smaller target

1. The aim is not to shoot precision shots but to suppress and neutralize the attacker with speed and general vital area precision along the central line, which is about 2.5 - 3 inches wide and the length of the torso.

1. Shot placement for a brain stem shot

Sequence of shooting from draw to stable stance and first shot:
Relaxed Correct grip

Clear holster Stance

Weapon in line with eyes (both eyes open)

Your mind should be occupied with the tactical movements of your opponent, not your sights unless targets are further than 10 -15 meters and you are preferably using a rifle and not your pistol.

It is very possible with practice to hit a target out to 20 meters with point aim, **but only do this in a war zone environment where you know all the people that are in front of you are combatants.** In a crowd situation, make sure you know **who is behind the target** and **use your sights** with the lower stance to **angle your shot upwards.**

Error in accuracy diagram (explanations follow):

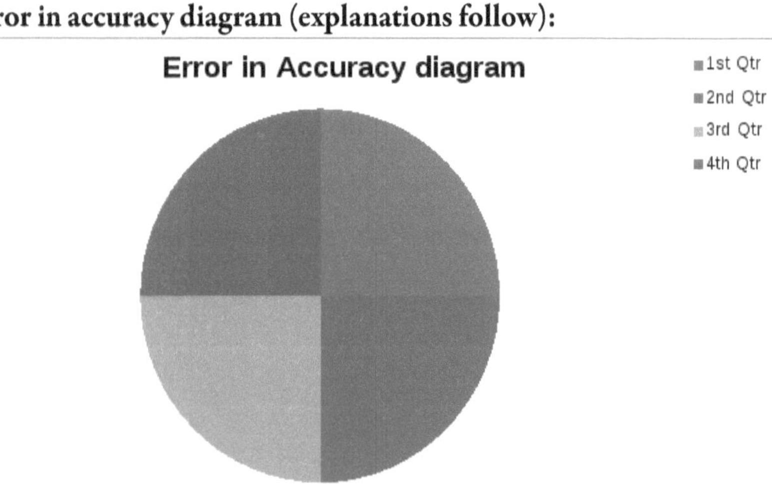

This is not an exhaustive list of corrections to inaccurate fire, just a guideline:

For the student to shoot the center mass where they are aiming takes proper grip control, trigger control, controlled tension and straight but fairly relaxed arms. The grip should be firm and you should try to keep it the same every time you draw – to get consistency close the gap between your palms and point the thumbs towards the target. The trigger control is a hooked finger that pulls straight back. The following areas drawn above indicate the area where the bullets will hit if there is an error in the shooting technique.

Note: Any bend in your arm will result in a tension correction in real combat where you will straighten your arm and then miss the target

1. The **Blue area** or 1st quarter can be pushing with the left hand, or incorrect sight picture where the front sight is slightly over to the right. Very seldom will the person have such long fingers that the right hand trigger finger goes so deep the shooter can pull the weapon slightly to the right but it is possible, depending on the type of weapon used, as some have a very short distance between trigger and grip.

2. The **Red area** or 2nd quarter can be a combination of anticipation and pushing with the left hand, or pulling with the left hand which can dip the front of the barrel. That's why a neutral grip that is firm but not too tight is preferable. If you keep the wrist firm you also allow a better control over the recoil and the weapon should come back to its starting position. When using other types of shooting stance, such as "the Weaver stance" or grip you will find that when adrenaline kicks in then the strong arm will straighten and you will shoot to the right side.

3. The **Green area** or 3rd quarter shots, if they run along the

line between the two quarters, can be squeezing the left hand fingers of the left hand grip when you fire and therefore pulling the weapon across to the left.

   a. **If you squeeze the left hand grip and anticipate it will go left and low.**

   b. **Squeezing the right hand grip can also cause the weapon to move to the left and anticipation moves the gun down so this can be a cause for shooting left and low, especially in a stress situation.**

   c. **Incorrect trigger control: finger is too deep and the side of the trigger finger is pushing the weapon to the left side.**

4. The **Purple area** or 4th quarter close to the line that runs between the 4th and 3rd quarter is normally the side of the finger on the trigger pushing the weapon across to the left. If the shot is higher than it could be the front sight is raised above the 'v' notch of the back sight just as you shoot i.e., it's a misaligned sight problem.

Note: shooting low in the red or green quarters can be anticipation of the shot and this happens a lot with people who have just started to learn how to shoot.

Note: It is important at this stage of the training to **integrate** the **mental aspects** (mindset) of combat shooting, to allow these things to become second nature e.g.

- Awareness (to see and understand your surroundings)
- Mindset (The attitude of personality at the point of contact / moment of attack)
- Mental tools (used to asses and guide your planning as you see and process your environment)

- Physical and mental preparation techniques (deep breathing allows a more relaxed body)
- Justification, predetermined attitude of what you are willing to do
- Add in scanning or checking after each engagement by utilizing 'z' or figure 8 techniques and then looking left and right.

By now, the draw should be smooth and the person should be focused on placing the weapon in front of them between their eyes and looking at the target. If you do not put the weapon between your eyes your brain has no point of reference, therefore you will not be able to point it accurately. If the weapon is in front of your eyes, you will have control of the natural pointing of the weapon (depth, up and down and side to side).

It will be important to focus on trigger control at this point. Do not jerk the trigger it should be a slow and controlled where possible.

Remember that a person is **not** always immediately incapacitated when shot, it is therefore important to consider bullet placement and keep focused on your assailant until they are out of the picture. Unless the dynamic situation demands you to move onto another target.

Once you have shot, you can bring the weapon close in to give you a stronger retention position. There is a double-handed strong retention position and a single-handed position.

Shooting in four directions while standing

Here it is important to master shooting in all four directions, as you have no idea where your assailants will be placed during a confrontation. You will initially do only do one direction at a time with turning.

These are:

1. Front
2. Quick turn to left
3. Quick turn to right
4. Turn to face backwards quickly with no side step yet. This means turning on the spot with just moving your feet

The first exercises are done in a **stationary stance standing** and only moving the feet slightly and this means you have to move the upper body and arm to shoot to the side or back. To handle close range (1 to 5 meters) attackers, the weapon is brought close to the body and fired from here, or punched out for targets that are further away.

The second exercises are done in a **stationary kneeling stance** only moving the knees slightly and this means you have to move the upper body and arm to shoot to the side or back.

These are:

1. Quick turn to face backwards; this requires turning the knees by putting one knee down first then lifting the other knee.
2. To shoot on the side of the raised knee requires pulling the weapon close and bending the left arm will allow you to shoot left without moving your legs if your left knee is up and you are a right-handed shooter then this is what you will do to shoot to the left.

3. Shooting to the open side or your right side means just turning the torso with arms extended this will allow you to move about 90 degree from the front shooting position.

Checking your environment

When you are in a combat environment you search your environment to look for:

Don't go into a combat environment without being mentally prepared

1. Extra attackers besides the person you just engaged.
2. You look for the enemy in a military or PSD situation.
3. To assess the possibility of where to move for cover (exit to escape).

Picture sequence showing engagement of a small steel plate (frame 1) then scanning with a Z pattern to the front (frames 2 and 3), pulling the weapon in (frame 4) and looking around the sides left and right (frames 5 and 6):

Note: Utilize peripheral vision

You will **only be able to use your peripheral if you train it,** as it does not come naturally in combat. In fact one of the stress responses is for the peripheral vision to diminish and one of the ways you know your training is kicking in is when your peripheral vision works when in a combat situation.

Checking your environment also includes the **quick peek** technique to establish who is around a corner. Remember where the enemy is (take a mental picture), make a mental note of what they are using, possible future cover, and assess if they are aware of you. The quick peek can also be a low peek then shoot high or a high peek and then shoot low, it's a only a fraction of a second but it makes a difference.

Points when scanning done correctly

1. Front and slightly to side of actual targets then 90degree to sides first
2. Pull weapon to strong retention and keep both hands on
3. As you will see from the pictures, you must keep your chin in as you are checking behind you for a potential attacker so you don't want to get knocked out
4. If you feel you need to move the weapon then move slightly to the side, but not too far off from front center line as theoretically this is where the main threat was coming from. Having said that there are no absolutes in combat and no rules so do what you feel you need to in the moment. This is for self-defense you don't have to consider your team mates

The right way to check your six

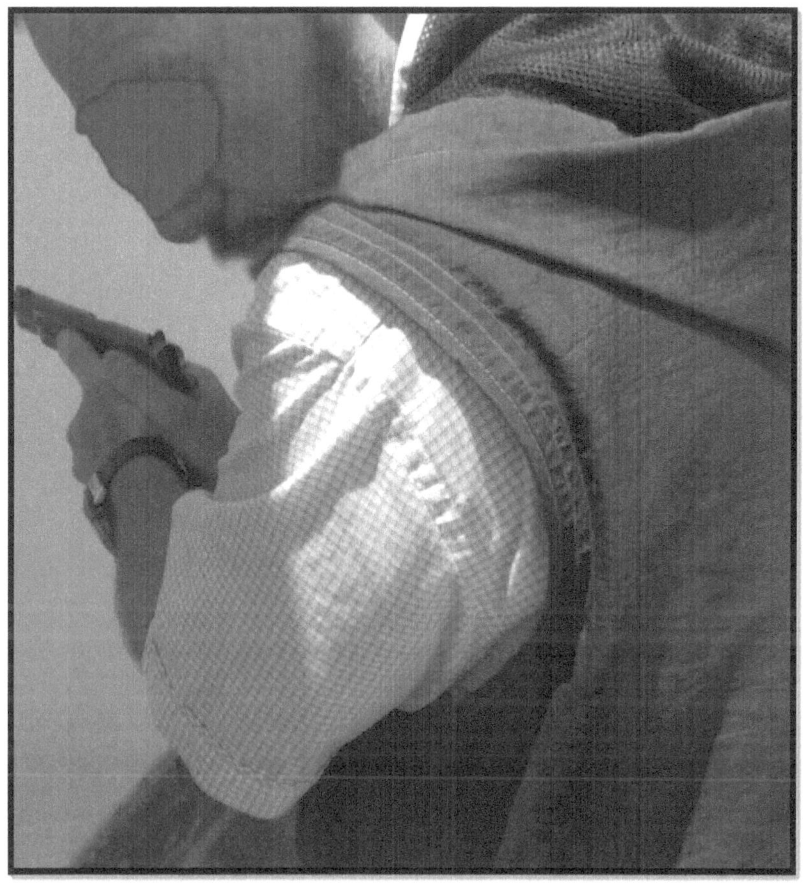

Mistakes made when doing your scan

1. Not checking the sides and back, as some people only check to the sides of the target they just engaged
2. Only holding the weapon with one hand, this is a very bad retention position if someone grabs at your weapon from a position of cover such as at a corner of a wall. Lifting your chin up so that any person behind you can knock you out. Do the most secure check you can don't take a chance that nobody is behind you as they can be very close
3. Taking your weapon out of line of your area of the main threat, which is directly in front
4. Not moving laterally when you check to the side and back; this is also to make you a hard target for someone standing behind you who could be a possible opponent.
5. Set aside training for scanning and don't do scanning in all the basic movement and techniques to save time only at an Elite level you might want to up the amount of training of your awareness

Side Note: Only move your weapon off main threat to front in the event you have made certain the threat to the front is neutralized or more of a threat materializes from another sector

The wrong way to check your six shown below

For the full version of this manual you can see on Amazon see below details the full version is 229 pages long:

Basic to Elite level Handgun

Author M Harland

On Amazon

Weapon carry techniques

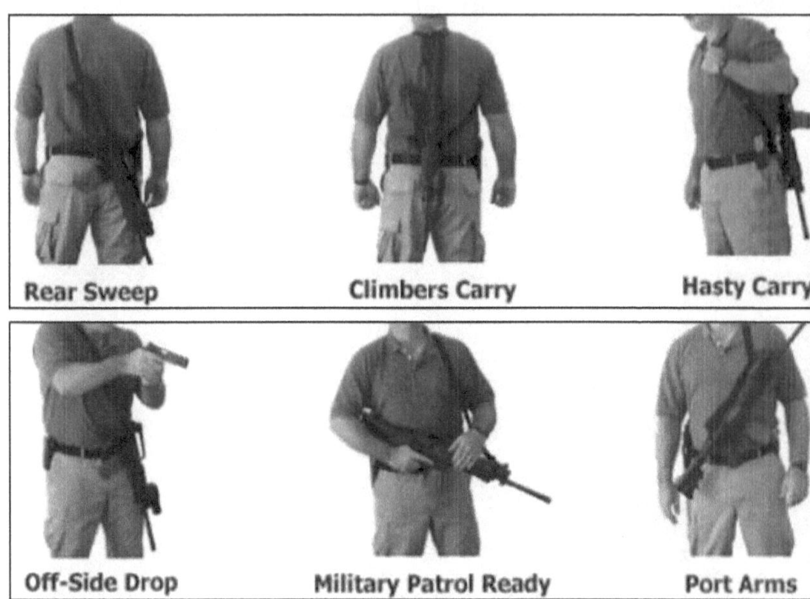

Best carry position for the combat rifle when in small teams is high port (barrel facing sky wards) as this negates most accidents, and if an accidental discharge happens then the round won't possibly ricochet off the ground into someone's legs. If you are operating on your own then it doesn't matter as it's only the enemy that you have to worry about.

Trauma bandage
No left side holsters available so pistol on right hip
AK
Blade

How to teach weapons training for combat

One of the most important aspects to teach a student is how to teach themselves, this is the **introspective principal**. This demands confidence on the side of the student. They should learn from their mistakes and think about solutions to problems they find in training when confronted with them, and this will also help to develop a *flexible mindset for combat*. Most of my students that have trained for 2 or more years understand this principle and apply it when we train in class and this helps them to self-correct where their understanding allows. This is only possible if you have explained why certain techniques work and how they work so the person develops an understanding of the actual reasons for doing a technique or not.

This is master level understanding and is never taught or explained or even mentioned, this can lead to the situation sometimes phrased as "when the student is ready, the master will appear!" This is due to the fact the student has enough experience to draw from that allows them to decide if a certain change will be beneficial or not. This is limited to the extent where the student has either less of a capacity to be introspective and or the background knowledge to make a decision and whether this would be a better or not. This is directly proportional to the instructor's combat knowledge of real life combat and less of a fictional understanding.

The subject of street fighting/war/battle can be made more difficult to teach because of the amount of disinformation out there in the public domain. The student is presented with so many options by this I mean systems, philosophies (view points) and instructors (with varied backgrounds and experience). Firstly the systems are varied and numerous and not all geared towards practical application this is borne out in reality when you have for instance a system like Capoeira being applied in MMA and the exponent loses. To a large extent it doesn't work in the street the reason for this is the time it takes to execute most of the techniques which are large flowery movements that fit into a dance more than real combat. So a person without real combat knowledge but extensive training in Capoeira might be under the impression that his system is good for real street combat without having tested it (having a few street fights will quickly sort this self-deception out).

Some systems were originally practiced for real combat, and then they were adapted for sports purposes, which left them *almost devoid of combative application*. This is one of the reasons so many different systems were tested in the MMA arena and some fell short and others grew in prominence. This doesn't mean all MMA fighting systems are applicable to the street because there are still rules in MMA and there are **no rules in the street**. This means in the street if a person grabs your arm for a lock, in MMA you can't punch them in the groin whereas in the street everything goes and this *nullifies some of the techniques* used in MMA therefore some techniques that are effective in the MMA arena are not effective in the street. Another example of this would be in a close-up situation you are not allowed to head butt, but in the street this is a devastating strike and can win a fight with one strike.

This leads to a split in systems that use some aspects of fighting and ignore the rest. Some fighting systems and this includes gun fighting systems, focus on the target shooting application of weapons training. This is important in combat but should be balanced with speed of shooting and intensity with the focus on both *speed and accuracy and mobility.* As with real street situations, you find yourself shooting at completely unique angles compared to your training if you do standard shooting training such as is done in any competition sport where the emphasis is on a standard shooting platform that might not even be possible to achieve in reality.

Some weapons fighting systems also only focus on the target practice aspect of pistol and leave out the close-in fighting that normally happens in self-defense situations. Leaving it almost devoid of real-life application. Pistol or rifle training for combat has to take into consideration the **stress of combat** and chaos or dynamic nature where you don't know what the enemy is going to do. The chaos and dynamic nature create situations where you have to shoot in a stance you haven't trained, or in close confines such a small room or vehicle. It is also the timing of a confrontation which causes confusion to the operator and because you are not ready you tend to fumble or miss the mark due to time constraints imposed by the attacker. This also means a favorable stance can't always be achieved.

Then we have systems that are completely impractical for self-defense but the student will only realize this once they get into a situation and either lose the fight or get killed (so that's a bit too late to help). Systems that rely purely on brute force can be effective but might be limited in the situation where a bit of finesse is needed such as in a confrontation with a person with a knife and or gun. Having said that once you have managed to get into range of the attacker to manipulate the weapon from them, only brute force and or lethal application of force (throat strike) will persuade the person, a person doesn't just give up their gun or knife. This is why it's so important to strike them in an area that causes enough incapacitation that will encourage them to release the knife or gun.

Both the blade and handgun have certain basic principles that need to be applied to win against them and this also applies to the rifle. The pistol defense such as disarming a pistol requires you to control the barrel (this causes a stoppage) then you need to disable the attacker by a strike (normally a groin kick, throat strike or neck area in general) after the strike you can more easily use leverage to try manipulate the weapon from the attacker's hand. It doesn't have to be in this sequence

– you can strike as you grab the barrel, just don't lose the grip on the barrel before you have caused a stoppage.

The secret is it must be fast, aggressive and efficient, sometimes aggression can be the only thing you need but if the person is strong then you will need technique to win. If you are too close to the enemy then you can execute your disarm of his weapon system, if you are too far from them try the zig zag running technique. If you are far enough then run because at about 10 meters most average shooters cannot hit a running target specially one that is moving erratically by this I mean side to side and up and down while running. This means the situation is dynamic if both the attacker and you are moving, which is most probable.

Then we have systems that rely on a **high level of skill** and manipulation of the weapon when trying to disarm the attacker. **The problem is trying to fit a slow technique that relies on fine motor skills** into an adrenaline pumping brute force attack at **high speed, it's just not going to work due to fine motor skills not working well when adrenaline is present.** This is one of the reasons Aikido doesn't work in the street. It might have stood a chance in the street if all your techniques were **practiced at street combat speeds and intensity** with varied angles and direction of attack. But it isn't and therefore it can't be used in real combat because of the unrealistic speed of attack and the type of attacks which are done from way out of normal combat range intensity and angles of attack etc.

You need to balance *skills* with both *brute force techniques*, and combine the ability to deal with the attacks that require a more delicate approach or fast light movements and attacks that require brute force; this is very difficult to teach and takes real skill and knowledge as an instructor.

As with all endeavors in life there will be your academics and there will be warriors. Not **many people** have **the warrior spirit** and determination to be really good; most **are looking for a quick**

solution (it does not exist, except in dreams and fantasy). Some are truly blessed to be both warriors and academically minded. Like with all sports or combat systems you have to **train hard** and **long** to be really good and if possible maintain them as they will deteriorate over time. Like with any sport or martial/fighting system, **the instructor's real-life experience** and understanding can accelerate learning or slow it down or even jeopardize the person's life as some systems will do due to their lack of real-life application.

When the student starts with their training, it is important to stress the *correct application of technique* as this allows the student to **fight efficiently**. Efficiency is the key and that means your technique must be correct and to know what the correct techniques is you have to have experience and know how. It should also be noted that technique in the *wrong context* could also be lethal, so stress this aspect as well.

You also need to stress the **ability to move** as this is the basis of all forms of combat and those that can't move lack a major aspect of fighting ability which translates into fighting strategy and ultimately into victory.

The only time a gunfight is going to be static is when you *shoot from very long range*, or you *shoot from cover* such as in a dugout, or from a building, it could also be from a vehicle if used as cover but it only applies to where the engine is as the rest doesn't give much real ballistic cover. Otherwise in a battle or SHTF type situation you will most probably be in the open patrolling. Walking to an objective or moving by vehicle which is not good if attacked as vehicles don't offer much cover except for engine compartment etc.

Visualization techniques

These are a training aid and not essential to success.

This is not meditation; it's visualization of what you can do in a combat situation and the winning mindset. This **reinforces the winning attitude** and settles the technique in your mind so that you can fully apply the technique with mental understanding and physical preparation when you have done the necessary repetitions manually.

1. Lie down in a relaxed environment.
2. Breathe deeply and close your eyes.
3. Consciously relax your muscles.
4. Visualization should be realistic as in what is humanly possible, and systematic as in correct sequence of events.
5. Realize that in reality you will have a certain amount of tension.
6. There will be confusion in a fight, so picture yourself focusing, relaxing and working through it to prevail.
7. You should see yourself drawing calmly, engaging each enemy as the situation presents itself, keeping all aspects of combat in mind, where the enemy is, the condition of your weapon, tactically who is the best person to engage first.
8. Allow your mind to instinctively come to the correct conclusion. This is what your mind is more than capable of doing.
9. Visualize as much detail as possible.

Stimulus and mental reaction programming

The student needs to develop an ability to overcome a natural fear response. This is done at different stages in the training. It replaces the normally fearful response with a confident one. This confident response is now part of the student's psychology once they have got to a point where what previously used to scare them does not do so anymore.

Start with basic things, like showing the student a real blade, and ask them how it makes them feel. If they sense fear then they should breathe deeply and focus on the thoughts of confidence and winning and **righteous anger**. Righteous anger is only possible if you are righteous and in right standing with GOD.

This exercise can be done every few months or weeks, as often as the instructor feels it is necessary. It should be increased in complexity so that the student develops a mindset of winning and is able to stop the debilitating effects of fear.

Fear can slow you down, make you weak, and sometimes even completely immobilize you, so you need to work through these things in your mind, changing your attitude to one of confidence and strength (fortitude).

Even when the student thinks they have overcome those fears and have the winning mindset then it is still important to maintain their mental skill and to put them in a place of stress so they can strengthen their attitude.

Negative stimuli for students

Ask the student what creates a negative thought or fear for the student.

1. It might be the sight of a blade
2. When the person sees a gun
3. It might be darkness and a strange person approaches them
4. Certain sounds, such as a gun cocking or a blade opening
5. It might be a person in the shadows with something in the hand (not necessarily a dangerous weapon).

This must then be overcome with a positive mindset through various exercises. This might take longer than you think as it takes a while to instill itself to where it becomes instinctive.

Summary of training principles

1. Teach only 1 or 2 techniques a day so the student can go off and learn/practice the subtleties at home, through repetition and using the introspective principle. If they don't have a lot of time at the training course to learn, then this can lead to problems if they do a technique incorrectly for too many repetitions as it could cause long term problems that will needed to be unlearned. Techniques have to be rehashed till the student understands it correctly.

2. Don't shoot lots of ammo, **do lots of technique** and **dry fire;** otherwise, it's a waste of money, time and energy. It is more advantageous to use less ammo and concentrate fully for 50 rounds worth of training than shoot 300 rounds and lose focus after just shooting 100 of them. A well-planned training program will cater for the basics which you should be good at for combat. This is magazine changes, stoppage drills, point aim and medium to long range shooting for combat, which would roughly be 100-300 meters which is what most combat ranges would be.

3. Explain, demonstrate and get the student to do the *technique slowly*,

    a. This is where you watch for any deviation from the technique. If you have explained it correctly then there won't be much deviation, you would also only add one new aspect at a time, minimizing mistakes.

    b. It would help to have the student be more *introspective* to learn from their mistakes and learn to adapt their technique as needed.

    c. As a training tool you can use video to show the person where they are going wrong, it's an excellent training tool I use it a lot.

4. Specific to combat is **movement training**, this is one of the most important aspects to teach to reach a really high level of combat efficiency and not necessary for sport shooting, unless the sport is a dynamic shooting discipline, probably like IDPA etc.

5. *Correct repetition of good technique* develops good shooting technique and fast access to this technique by your cerebellum. Sometimes called muscle memory, but probably has more to do with the neural pathways than muscles.

   a. These pathways are probably better developed than other neural pathways, the information to react and make the movement possible is also already established and easier to access. These pathways it seems can be improved and increased with use, correct nutrition and rest.

   b. Specific muscle development could also play a role as it takes very specific muscles to grip a weapon whether a handgun or rifle. These specific muscles need to strengthen and the ligament attachments for specific muscles also need to strengthen, and the combination of the specific strength and neural pathways having been established is what makes for the speed and accuracy. The muscles are primed and in peak physical conditioning allowing the body to use to their improved state to the utmost to achieve speed and accuracy.

   c. ***Efficiency of the techniques*** will also play a major role, developing and maintaining this is what matters. You want to be fast, accurate and move with efficiency, which means relaxed power in the case of striking and relaxed movement and accuracy in the case of shooting.

6. **Develop <u>intensity</u> slowly**, over months and if time allows **over years,** as this allows you to focus on your technique and *not lose your efficiency*. Efficiency is normally directly related to speed, so use the introspective principal to correct your technique. This is done by thinking through every step of the move you are trying to accomplish and self-correcting where necessary.

7. *Include stress* when the student has a *good grasp of the basics*. This may take up to 6 months to develop, not 6 days as some might think. This is contrary to what has been thought and indirectly believed for some time by many instructors, which is possibly brought about by the short course of 2-3 days being so numerous and prevalent in modern day teaching of any combat discipline.

   a. If you stress the student too early, they will subconsciously ingrain incorrect response and a breakdown of technique. This in turn will slow them down and make them less accurate than they should be, this is not so much a conscious thought but a subconscious one.

   b. When inducing stress do it *incrementally*, too fast and you break the person down, too slow and you take a vital aspect combat out of their grasp, affecting their combat efficiency.

   c. Monitor the student so you don't make it too hard, especially in the initial stages, as this causes a subconscious thought pattern that associates all combat with fear and trepidation as well as a weakening of the mind and body due to the over active adrenaline surge and body tensing up.

   d. Build it up to as close to real combat stress as possible but don't forget **SAFETY.** If done properly, this will take months if training weekends once a week for 2-4 hours. Like all things in life, the individual has a limited capability to adapt to stress, their upbringing will affect this to some extent as some individuals that are brought up in a tough environment will tend to be more resilient.

    e. Don't stress the student excessively without ***giving them the tools*** to deal/manage with the stress first. Teach them how to deal with the stress using mindset, this means the stress induced is only going to teach the person to lose control in the moment of combat if it is not accompanied by the tools to deal with them.

8. You have to include mindset and explain the importance of attitude and how being relaxed in a confrontation affects your performance. Constantly reinforcing the mindset is very important to performance in combat. Cultivating this is a long-term goal as it's not quick to change an ingrained mindset that took years to instill from youth. Only constant reinforcement will enable you to change this.

Learn from others mistakes because some mistakes are deadly and final, don't be a statistic.

Searching the Premises for an IED

The search team should be given an idea of what they are searching for. If the modus operandi of the terrorist organization is to place explosives, then this will be the primary reason for the search. This will also give some idea of where to look and what they will be looking for.

The same principles for a vehicle search are applied to for premises. If the premises are secured correctly there is much less chance of an IED being placed? It is not always possible to secure a venue as the venue may not belong to the principal or you may not have the manpower to secure it.

As always, it is better to use professionals to search a venue by using dogs trained to search for explosives. If possible, ask the caretaker or people that work at the venue to assist and tell you if there is anything out of place.

Before you can start the search, familiarize yourself with the types of devices that will be used and how they are made.

For any premises you'd have to start by first searching the area around the building. An explosive device can have an effect to 100 meters (depending on its size). Searching around the building you would normally look at places where an explosive device can be placed, such as vehicles, dustbins, pot plants, in bushes, in or behind electrical appliances such as billboards, manhole and anything else that can contain a device.

Searching inside the venue is more time consuming and difficult as there is many fixtures and places to put an explosive device.

When searching, use all your senses, including hearing, smell and sight. If everything is quiet and you are close enough and the terrorists were stupid enough to use a large clock as a timer for a device, then it could be possible for you to hear the thing ticking. Explosive substances such as plastic explosive have a distinctive smell as well, as do certain substances used in improvised explosives. Any smell that is unusual should be investigated.

When looking you should be searching for a device that will have some sort of triggering mechanism, or timer, a power source, detonator and the explosives itself. To be effective in a building, the device would have to be relatively large if it was an improvised explosive device. It would have to measure at least eight to 12 inches in length with a diameter of four to six inches and weighing two to eight kilograms (this will do damage in a large room).

For military explosives such as C4, Semtex, PE4, TNT, the charge is normally cased in a specifically designed housing. This gives them a distinctive look and you should be familiar with the more commonly used ones. Plastic explosive can also be molded to any desired shape, therefore realize that an object could be filled with plastic explosive and used as a device.

The search will also include the detection of surveillance devices such as bugs. These can be placed in almost any conceivable housing such as pens, clocks, lights, briefcases and anything big enough to house it.

It would be best to have a person to oversee the searching and he would have a search card that allows one to tick off every area as once it has been searched and marked.

Remember that any premises or vehicle that has been searched should be secured until the arrival of the principal.

A thorough search should be done on all areas that are close to the place the principal will be sitting or positioned.

During the search of premises, you should also be aware of weapons that may have been placed to be accessible to someone at the time your principal arrives.

You should also take note of people that stand out and that have no reason for being on the premises.

All people involved in the searched should be adequately briefed as to the responsibilities of each person searching. The area should be divided up into responsibilities according to their function such as dogs that can search a large perimeter or garden. By allocating rooms to pairs of Close Protectors charged with searching the premises, to make the situation easier. The search team must know how much time they must do the search, when the principal arrives, etc.

Always give yourself enough time to have a venue properly searched in high threat situations with adequate resources to secure the venue afterwards. Pre-planning according to the itinerary given to you by the principal will give you the opportunity to assess which buildings need to be searched and to what level they need to be searched.

Common Placement Areas for IED's

All places where an explosive device will have the most effect and this is normally where the most people will be killed:

1. Halls
2. Conference rooms
3. Bar area
4. Escalator or lift if it is easiest to place there
5. Parking

Basic Equipment you will Need to Search a Premises

1. Overalls
2. Torch: have a large and small one for tight corners
3. At least 2 types of screwdrivers
4. Multipurpose knife
5. Stethoscope to check if a wall is hollow
6. Magnifying glass to check for listening devices
7. Basic radio FM detector for the most common FM bugs, if this is part of your purpose
8. Metal detector for metal parts of a device if you suspect one built into a wooden table or chair.

Search Procedure

1. Switch off all electronic devices and the electricity supply to the building (where practical and possible). Switch off all pagers, radios and cell phones.
2. Don't forget to search outside the venue out to 100 meters if you are in the Middle East or a country known for terrorism where they use large IED's.
3. Check pot plants, drains, sign boards if they are hollow, bushy areas, drainpipes, parked cars (or they must be removed), outside lights and dust bins.
4. The search must be systematic, working away from the outside of the building inward. Each room that is searched will be searched from ground level to waist-high and then from waist high to ceiling. The roof can be checked last.
5. At ground level to waist height, you can start at the door, working your way clockwise and ending at the door again.
6. Keep in mind what you are looking for. Once something has been searched, mark it off with chalk or tape.
7. Remember to have a co-coordinator and the janitor or someone who is a handyman that can identify the things that are out of place.
8. Look for signs that indicate that an IED or surveillance device was placed such as a place where you would normally find dust and is now clean, any presence of wires, grease marks, tape, peg, foil, etc.
9. If you have limited time and are not sure about a certain room you can minimize the risk of placement of IEDs and surveillance devices by taking some of the equipment out that is not necessary, such as furniture and appliances.
10. If the venue has been searched and you are still not sure whether it is safe, and time does not allow, then change the

room or the venue.

11. If the threat level dictates, you may have to search everything including switches, light bulbs, and all fittings.

12. Remember in certain instances you may even have to search underneath the floorboards. This will be a time-consuming procedure so allow more than enough time to do the search.

13. The coordinator will have the relevant telephone numbers of the bomb squad and other services such as police to cordon the area off if a device is found.

14. When searching a toilet area remember to search the whole area including the working parts of the toilet and the bowl where the water is stored for flushing.

15. Check the roof. If it is a false ceiling, go through the trap door and remember to take a large torch with you.

16. Do not stop searching if you find a device – carry on and search the whole place thoroughly.

17. Once the search is complete you should now **place security** to stop someone from entering and placing device. Secure the whole area inside and outside.

If anything is found, apply the **four C's:** confirm, clear, cordon and control.

Report the incident to the relevant authority if the police are not already on the premises.

Example of shockwave from a VBIED (notice the white shockwave moving out from the blast, visible along the ground):

ADDR: 1   - V1.64

ADDR: 1   - V1.64

ADDR: 1 - V1.64

ADDR: 1 - V1.64

ADDR: 1 - V1.64

ADDR: 1 - V1.64

ADDR: 1 - V1.64

ADDR: 1 - V1.64

Effective Locations for IED's

Areas where it will damage valuable equipment or places of strategic value:

1. Areas where computers are kept such as the mainframe/central servers
2. Offices where the company's files are kept (incendiary device)
3. Areas where large sums of money are kept
4. Medical facilities of forces opposing the terrorists such facility belonging to UK, US, European countries. Specially facilities in third world countries.
5. All areas of value
6. Ammo dumps
7. Logistical bases
8. Water systems
9. Electrical power plants

How to Reduce the Risk of IED or Explosive Being Introduced

1. Evaluate the target area
2. Asses weak points
3. Decide on a plan of action /strategy
4. Strengthen weak points
5. Apply strategy

Strategy to Reduce Risk of Explosives Being Placed

1. Know what you are protecting against
2. Use undercover agents/operators trained in observing unusual behavior
3. Do advance and plan accordingly
4. Control all entrances out to 200 meters from the venue, when possible
5. Install vehicle stoppers
6. Secure the perimeter
7. Check the guest list
8. Control internal perimeter with surveillance camera (change monitors every hour)
9. Restrict the number of people entering the premises
10. Search all official and unofficial vehicles
11. Control visitors' movement
12. Lock all area not being used and control access to peripheral areas
13. Have good communications between security forces and access control
14. Use dogs at the entrances and particle detectors at the gates for pedestrian access
15. Train all relevant staff

Training Staff to Counter IED's

Training staff in access control to limit the introduction of IED's

1. You may not stop someone from placing an IED, but you can make it very difficult for him or her by forcing him or her to be more careful and maybe they will choose an easier place to hit.
2. Show and put-up pictures of terrorist weapons IED's and commonly used grenades, limpid and other explosive devices.
3. You could explain to them the approximate size that an effective improvised explosive device will be 12 inches long up to four inches wide and approximately four kilograms and weight. This is a large object, and it will be difficult to introduce it on to the premises by carrying it without being noticed.
4. It has been procedure in the past to carry the IED on to the premises in a nondescript bag. They will use a bag that will not stick out in the surrounding environment. The person will normally leave it next to an object out of the view of people so that it is not noticed
5. The staff or access control should know to report immediately to head of security or OC in charge of the close protection and they should establish as fast as possible to which the bag belongs.
6. The person who tries to introduce the explosive device on to the premises will certainly show some signs of stress and apprehension, explained to them the warning signs and how to read them if they notice someone.
7. The above procedure is applicable for a venue where all the bags are not such.
8. Explained to the access control that if they are attempting to

minimize the introduction of IED, they should be looking for an object which is relatively large, as explained above to be effective it would have to be quite or large. For a grenade to be affective it would have to be in a crowded place.

Actions on Finding an IED

The following are steps you should NOT take if you find a device:

1. Cover it up unless it is with a bomb blanket
2. Put it in a pool if it can damage the structural integrity of the building that the IED is in
3. Touch it (as it may go off if it has a sensitive switch)
4. Call on your radio next to it
5. Close the doors and windows. (As this will cause the glass to turn into shrapnel and contained the blast making it even more effective)

For some unknown reason if you do pick the device up (not very clever/ unless you are very brave) and it did not detonate then place it in an open area.

Searching for Surveillance Devices

The search must be done systematically so no areas are left out. It will normally start from the ground and work upwards. A manual search is very time consuming and difficult because you can hide surveillance devices in almost anything. Using a device that picks up the signal from a bug is faster but must be applied properly to get the best result. It will also help to get a detector that can pick up the sophisticated devices you are likely to find if the opposition has the money. Before searching an area, it would help to know who the possible perpetrators are, as this will give you an idea of where to search and what you are looking for.

Terrorists will have a limited budget but may still be able to get sophisticated devices. You can also expect low-level devices (FM frequency devices and devices bought 'over the counter'). First world countries' intelligence agencies may use the latest technology and go through a lot of effort to place devices so you may not find all the bugs by doing a manual and equipment search. Some of the bugs may only be activated when the phone is picked up or when someone speaks so they will not give off any signal and hardwire devices pick up the signal directly from the line so you will not pick up waves in the air.

The area is split into sections from the bottom: feet to hip, hip to eye, eye to roof and roof itself.

Do not deny your sixth sense – if you feel something, act on it.

When searching consider how the people will install the device because they must take certain points into consideration e.g.

1. Good acoustic pick-up: the sound must be clear and not distorted or interfered with by other sounds.
2. Adequate RF signal propagation: the aerial should be placed so it is effective for a receiver to pick it up.
3. Good concealment.
4. Proximity: it must be positioned close enough to the people

who are being bugged to be effective. This means in the range of a microphone and within the device's ability to send to a receiver. This could be 50 to 100 meters for some FM devices and up to 500 meters for sophisticated ones.

5. Keep in mind covert cameras can be monitored from the Internet from anywhere in the world.

From the suitable places to install a device, the installer must determine where the center of conversation will be and the likely disturbances from appliances such as radios, fans, running bath water, etc. The device must be installed as far from such disturbances as possible.

Other factors that affect what sort of device is placed are **time on target.** This will determine if it is a throw away device put in a pot plant, placed on a high cupboard, or dropped in a wastebasket. It may also be a sophisticated device, which takes more time to install.

Take into consideration the ideal way to place an antenna is vertically to get better range; if it is placed horizontally, it loses range.

Search Procedure

The area is split in sections from the bottom feet to hip, hip to eye, eye to roof and roof itself.

Do not deny your sixth sense, if you feel something act on it.

When searching consider how the people will install the device because they must take certain points into consideration when placing surveillance device and these are:

Good acoustic pick-up: the sound must be clear and not distorted or interfered with by other sounds.

Adequate RF signals propagation, the aerial should be placed so it is affective for the receiver to pick it up.

Good concealment, it must be hidden so it will not be found.

Proximity, it must be positioned close enough to the people who are being bugged to be effective. This means in the range of the microphone and within the devices ability to send to the receiver. This could be 50 to 100 meters for some FM devices and up to 500 meters for sophisticated devices.

Keep in mind covert cameras' can be monitored from the Internet from anywhere in the world.

From the suitable places to install the device the installer has now to determine where the center of conversation will be and the likely disturbances from appliances such as radios, fans, bath water running and others. The device must be installed as far from the disturbances as possible.

Other factors that affect what sort of device is placed are **time on target for the enemy surveillance.** This will determine if it is a throw away put in a pot plant, placed on a high cupboard or dropped in a wastebasket. It may also be a sophisticated device, which takes more time to install.

Take into consideration the ideal way to place an antenna for a FM bugging device is vertical to get range; if it is placed horizontally, it loses range its effectiveness

Picture of a briefcase with surveillance device/bug detector:

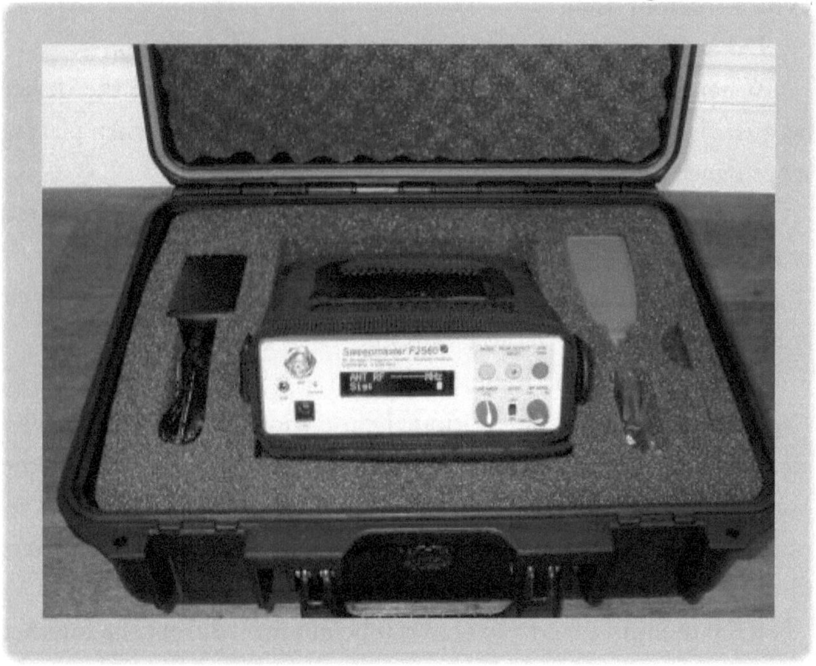

Example Devices and Preferred Placement Positions for Devices

1. Pre-built wall plug devices are obviously plugged in the wall.
2. TX-703 placed on curtains, blinds or draperies.
3. TX-755 used in junction box to be placed by an electrician.
4. Unitel 135 can monitor up to 4 target areas, record and monitor.
5. FM bugs are cheap and have good life span; can be placed anywhere
6. Audio drill to penetrate wall; requires access to a wall.
7. A tube microphone is used in a shared junction box.
8. A high impedance acoustic pick up is used on walls.

Example of surveillance devices that you could find in a room (venue):

Common Places to Hide Surveillance Devices (bugs)

1. Pot plants
2. Lighters
3. Matchbox
4. Inside electrical plugs (can be bought over counter at spy shop)
5. Desktop ornaments
6. Behind pictures, mirrors
7. Under and inside furniture
8. Curtains, in the seam
9. Roof, if it is a false ceiling
10. Drilled into a wall from the outside (security forces, police, and special forces)
11. Air vents, but only if they are not used as they may be too noisy
12. Any wooden structure that can be hollowed out
13. Light fittings and switches
14. Plug points/outlets
15. Under or in chairs and tables
16. Behind the headboard of a bed

Other Devices Used to do Surveillance on your Principal

1. Cell phones, tapping into the network
2. Shotgun microphone, directional
3. Hyper bowl amplifies sound, directional
4. Laser that picks up conversational vibration from a window, used on offices for industrial espionage
5. Directional devices as small as a cigarette box, used in e.g., a restaurant environment
6. Wire taps (used on phones) connected to tape recorder
7. Hardwire systems used by counter terrorist units to monitor a hostage taker through a wall.

Mains powered transmitter:

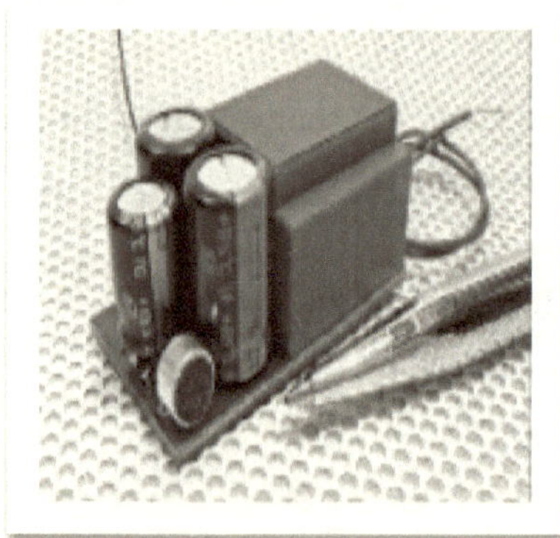

UHF Miniteltx transmitter:

Mains powered transmitter:

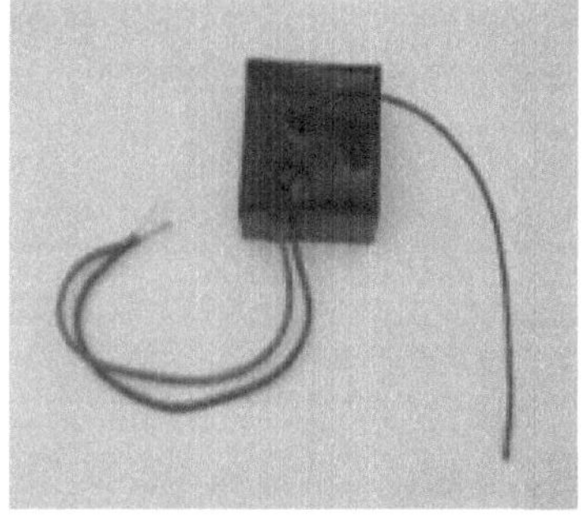

Pictures of mini-GPS tracker can be attached to vehicles:

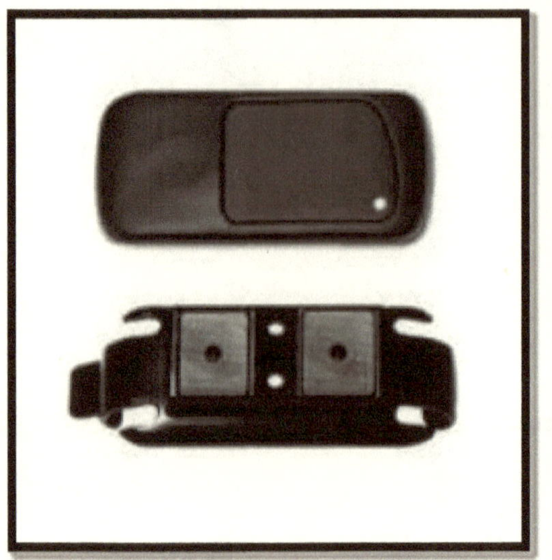 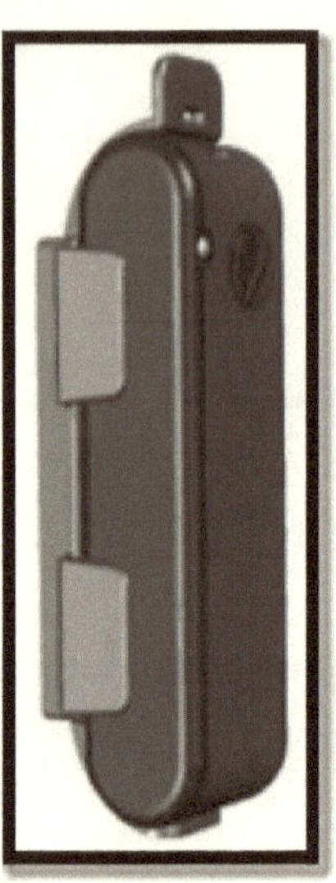

Car video camera KDBV (this cannot be installed covert unless the person is deceived into believing it is something else):

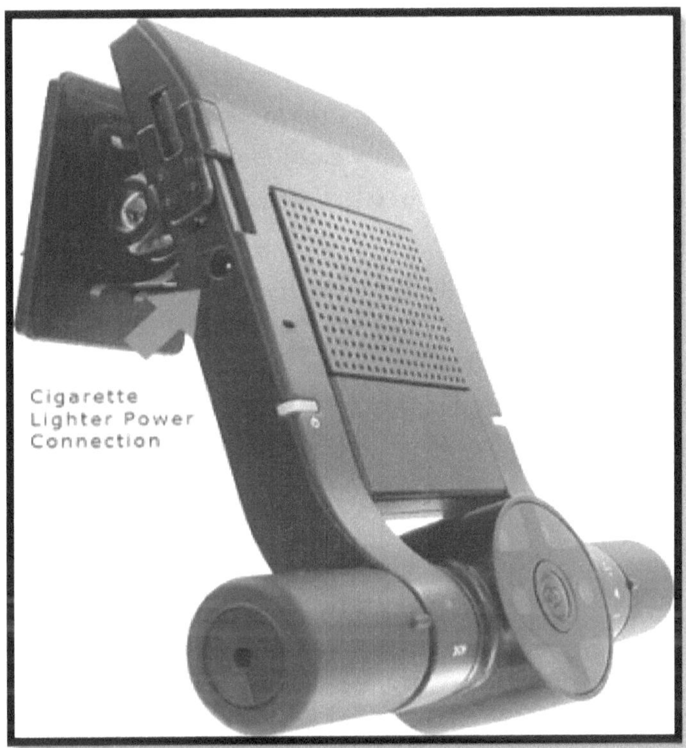

When time is not available to the civilian CP and the check must be cursory then you can inspect the most obvious areas such a plug points phones and other likely places. What you should look for is excessive damage to the screws from being taken out and replaced.

Places where the paint was damaged to access any area where you feel someone would put a device such as air vents (not normally mechanical ones as they would make too much noise to be effective) the combined damaged to screws and paint means the cover was opened more than just a few times. This could be just maintenance, but most high-class hotels won't have damaged appliances or screws or paint.

When doing a cursory check, you can also remember the point made above about what are the constraints for the person placing the device. This will help you narrow down quickly the most likely areas to search if you are in a hurry. Where is the most likely place the principal will sit so depending on the sophistication of the dice it has to be in that device acceptable range for effectiveness?

Another quick fix is to employ very good counter measures that interfere or stop (block) signals such as for cell phone bugs. The devices meant to serve as counter measures for surveillance will most likely only work for unsophisticated devices and not the government type device the US, Germany, France or UK would use.

Equipment Used to Search for Surveillance Devices

1. Correct clothes, overalls or other comfortable clothes
2. Wide range of screw drivers Allan keys and wrench
3. Fiber optic device for small areas hard to open or reach
4. Torch very bright white light
5. Stethoscope can be used to assess the walls but if the hard wire device was placed properly, you might not hear any hollow sound. Sometimes other devices are also placed in the wall such as small camera, but this will only work if concealed in some way
6. Small mirror for searching seats, behind cupboards etc.
7. Tape to mark areas that have been search and cleared, use any type of marker you feel comfortable with, but it must be visible and not confused with other marks / indicators left
8. Optional, multipurpose knife
9. Magnifying device

Technology Used in Bug Sweeps

The following technologies should only be used by a professional because of the problems that will be found in determining real bugs from just an electrical interference:

1. Frequency scanners (see example Figure 1 below) are used in a technical search. These can be basic types that are handheld and then the more sophisticated ones that scan most of the frequencies and ranges. The more sophisticated the more it will cost. These will locate bugs that emit a signal not devices that have been put off

2. **Millimeters** for general measurements

3. **Time-domain reflect meter** (TDR) for testing integrity of telephone lines and other communication cables

4. **Frequency scanner** with a range of antennas and filters for checking the electromagnetic spectrum for signals that should not be there

5. **Oscilloscope** for visualization of signals

6. **Spectrum analyzer** and **vector signal analyzer** for more advanced analysis of signals

7. **Nonlinear junction detector** (NLJD) for detection of hidden electronics

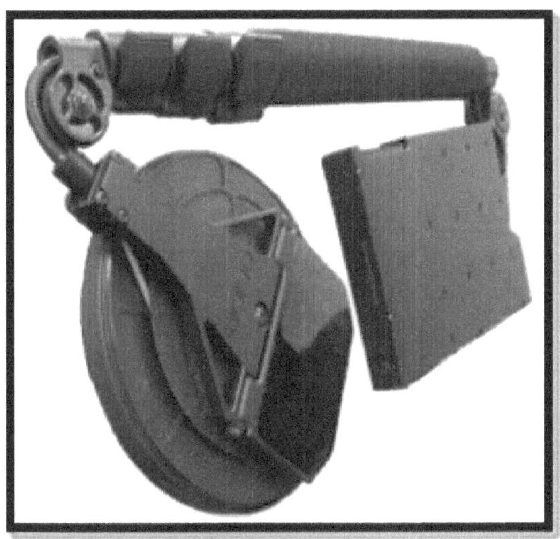

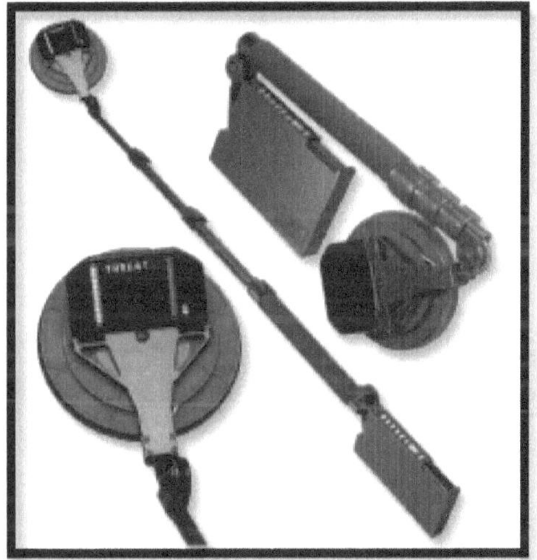

1. Portable **x-ray** machine for checking the inside of objects and walls.
2. **Computer security devices** and tools for computer-related threats. This might be software related or a key such as a USB key to start the computer.
3. **Tools for manual disassembling of objects** and walls in

order to visually check their content. This is the most important, most laborious, least glamorous and hence most neglected part of a check.

4. RF signal detector (frequency counter)

1. Frequency scanner

a. Detects digital and analogue signals
b. 16 Section bar graph to show RF signal strength
c. Selectable detection ranges: 1 GHz/2.8Ghz
d. 1 GHz range: 30 MHz to 0.8 GHz
e. GHz range: 500 MHZ to 2.8 GHz

f. Sensitivity adjustment
g. Hold switch to lock display
h. Low battery indicator
i. Sensitivity of less than 5mV
j. 15 dBm maximum input
k. 9V DC 300mA rechargeable battery power
l. Size: 33/4" x 2 3/4" x 1 1/4

It is important to remember to place a guard, so the place is not compromised after searching.

Don't miss out!

Visit the website below and you can sign up to receive emails whenever Mike Harland publishes a new book. There's no charge and no obligation.

https://books2read.com/r/B-A-BCLG-FPMVB

Connecting independent readers to independent writers.

Also by Mike Harland

Personal Security Detail Operations
Personal Security Detail Operations Book 1
Personal Security Detail Operations Book 2
Personal Security Detail Operations Book 3
Personal Security Detail Operations Book 4

The Fighting Rifle
The Fighting Rifle book 1
The Fighting Rifle Book 2
The Fighting Rifle Book 3

Standalone
Personal Protection And Body Guarding Manual

www.ingramcontent.com/pod-product-compliance
Lightning Source LLC
Chambersburg PA
CBHW031533150726
47990CB00001B/158